AMERICANS IN TRANSITION

LIFE CHANGES AS REASONS FOR ADULT LEARNING

CAROL B. ASLANIAN
HENRY M. BRICKELL

with the assistance of MARSHA DAVIS ULLMAN

WITHDRAWN

College Entrance Examination Board, New York, 1980

HIEBERT LIBRARY
Fresno Pacific College - M. B. Seminary
Fresno, Calif. 93702

20596

Publication of this book has been made possible by a grant from the Exxon Education Foundation.

The College Entrance Examination Board is a nonprofit membership organization that provides tests and other educational services for students, schools, and colleges. The membership is composed of more than 2,500 colleges, school systems, and education associations. Representatives of the members serve on the Board of Trustees and advisory councils and committees that consider the Board's programs and participate in the determination of its policies and activities.

Copies of this study may be ordered from College Board Publication Orders, Box 2815, Princeton, New Jersey 08541. The price is $10.75. Editorial inquiries concerning this study should be directed to Editorial Office, The College Board, 888 Seventh Avenue, New York, New York 10019.

Copyright © 1980 by College Entrance Examination Board. All rights reserved.

Printed in the United States of America.

ISBN: 0-87447-127-3

Cover photo credits:
Top: Alon Reininger, from De Wys.
Middle: Myron Wood, from Photo Researchers, Inc.
Bottom: H. Armstrong Roberts, Inc.

"No doubt the greatest opportunities for self-renewal
and new growth occur at those periods of life
when one's role changes."

—*John Gardner*

CONTENTS

FOREWORD

Although this report is focused particularly on adult education, the title reflects its broader implication: that one of the subtle but significant current changes in the American circumstance involves what is happening to the traditional sequence of major "transitions" in people's lives.

Until recently, this sequence was remarkably simple and uniform. Almost everyone went to school at age 6, took at one long sitting all the formal education he or she would ever get, moved directly from that to a "lifetime job" in either marketplace or home, and then retired at age 65 to rust. The three transition points came abruptly and passed quickly. The passages, accepted as functions of age and as beyond individual control, were considered so automatic that little or no institutionalization of responsibility for handling them developed. This worked well as far as meeting the needs of a burgeoning economy was concerned, and there were few individual complaints.

None of this is any longer true. The effects of a confluence of disparate developments — technological, social and economic, and political — include a crumbling of what was either the comforting stability or the enervating rigidity, perhaps both, of the traditional life pattern. This change is reflected particularly in the increasing frequency, duration, and complexity of people's movements from one holding pattern to another.

The child's first passage, from exclusively parental to dispersed responsibility, takes now a variety of forms. The next transition point, from school to work, has become almost an emergency area, characterized in part by 15 to 50 percent unemployment rates among various groups of 16- to 20-year olds. Lifetime jobs are now rarities. As technology creates more and more specialized occupations and obliterates old crafts, people change careers three, four, or even more times. Women's combining career motherhood with career something else creates a whole new set of transitions. At what used to be the final passage point, the sudden statutory scuttling of mandatory retirement at age 65 reflects political realization that the fastest growing age group of voters and taxpayers is rethinking the sufficiency of security alone.

Yet to approach and appraise these developments in terms only of concern and alarm would be to reflect the congenital timidity about change in any of its forms. What is happening at these passage points is at least arguably more a reflection of new liberation of the human spirit and individual potential than of frustration. It is clear only that with so many Americans now almost suddenly involved in so many and such different kinds of transitions, the traditional institutional structures, developed essentially around the service of continuums of the individuals' activities, are inadequate.

The College Board, however, is one of the few institutions that has dealt with transitions for a long time, and with widely recognized effectiveness. It brings a depth of experience, developed in connection with the movement of young people between secondary and postsecondary schools, to its Future Directions for a Learning Society project. This book, *Americans in Transition,* by Carol Aslanian and Henry Brickell, appears as one of the first products of the broader FDLS efforts.

The book proceeds from a synthesis of current knowledge about adult interests and motivations, as far as career advancement is concerned, with special emphasis on attitudes regarding renewed formal education. It examines the correlation between the current return-to-school movement and various social and economic developments. Asking "why do adults learn," the authors draw from their interviews with some 2,000 men and women an important central conclusion: that most adult decisions to seek educational renewal are clearly and directly related to significant changes in their lives — changes affecting their careers, family situations, health, religion, or leisure opportunities. Going back to school is less significantly a transition in itself than a consequence of some other change, actual or anticipated, in individual circumstance.

This study will be welcomed by architects of transition because it illuminates the key motivational aspects of a development — the return of adults to formal education — which has been occurring so rapidly that we have been taking it generally as it shows up in a head count of the new enrollees. What emerges from this deeper analysis is a pattern of serious intent and defined purpose that permits responsive adult educational curriculum development.

This kind of information will be invaluable, too, in developing a more rational and effective political science and institutional architecture of transition. The tendency has been, and remains today, to try to buy ourselves out of the problems that develop at these passage points. Not knowing anything better to do when someone's job ends, we put up money — for unemployment insurance or social security. If it isn't enough or when it runs out, the individual is left to go the rest of the way alone. We are only beginning to realize that there will have to be an affirmative action element in transition policy; that just providing the individual with money may well prove both costly and ineffective, and that renewed educational opportunity may be the central element in an alternative and more constructive policy.

Another reasonable inference from this record is that a transition policy can be developed more effectively at the state — and particularly the local level — than at the federal level. Since individuals moving back and forth between what traditionally have been considered separate institutional sovereignties are involved, the effective implementation of this policy requires new forms of collaboration. At the federal level, this only can be between departments of a government remote from the scene; locally it can bring together the employers for whom the individuals were, are, or will be working, the schools they turn to for refurbishing or enlarging their skills, and the community agencies that ought to be involved. The principles of pluralism have a special applicability when it comes to handling transitions, and these principles are more easily and effectively implemented by people who know each other and who know, too, the particular educational, work, service, and recreational opportunities that are available. Increasing experience with various kinds of local community education-work council confirms this potential.

Most of all, this book suggests the critical importance of recognizing the prospects as well as the problems involved here. Transition policy will find its vitalizing force in the eventual recognition of the new growth opportunities, for individuals, institutions, and the community as a whole, as more flexible life patterns open up. Small private colleges facing serious enrollment declines with fewer young people coming along will realize, partly because the alternative is extinction, that adults living just across the campus borders want, need, and are going to get, one place or another, what these colleges already offer or could provide with very little adjustment. In broader terms, a society worried about reported limits to its growth will recognize that while Americans in transition are typically individuals encountering uncertainty and often difficulty, the enlargement of their opportunities represents a new frontier for the democracy's expansion.

Willard Wirtz
Chairman, National Institute
for Work and Learning

PREFACE

For more than 75 years the College Board has worked toward improving access to higher education for the nation's youth. For more than 20 years the Board has been extending its services to adults desiring further training and preparation in both traditional and nontraditional settings. The Board's programs and activities for adults have included the Commission on Nontraditional Study, which examined and promoted innovative ways for adults and others to continue their learning; the College-Level Examination Program (CLEP), which offers more than 50 examinations through which adults can demonstrate their knowledge of college-level subjects learned outside the classroom; and the Office of Library Independent Study and Guidance Projects, which exhibited ways in which the existing resources of public libraries could be used for meeting the needs of adult independent learners.

For the past three years, the College Board has been sponsoring the nation's most intense search for future strategies to serve the needs of adult learners: the Future Directions for a Learning Society (FDLS) Program. Funded by the Exxon Education Foundation, FDLS has, in addition, gained support for its activities from the Sears-Roebuck Foundation, the

United States Office of Education, the Fund for the Improvement of Postsecondary Education, and the College Board itself. Overall, FDLS focuses on advancing knowledge in the field of adult learning, providing information on the needs of adult learners and of the agencies, institutions, and others that serve them; promoting improved public policy and public understanding about lifelong learning; and establishing services to improve adult access to learning opportunities.

In recent years, there has been an enormous increase in adult learning—both formal and informal. Adults today constitute more than half of all full-time and part-time college students and will make up well over half the total in the years to come. Millions more are learning at their places of employment, through private lessons, in local school districts, in their churches, through their professional associations, and in voluntary community organizations. Even more are learning on their own through television, libraries, museums, correspondence courses, and other sources.

This rapid growth in adult learning has not been well understood. Why has the rate of participation in learning exceeded the rate of population growth? Why does adult learning grow in bad economic times as well as good? If we had a better understanding of the dynamics underlying adult learning—the interplay of psychological, social, and economic forces that drive adult learning—perhaps we could account for the current rate of growth.

The purpose of the FDLS study reported in the book was to identify the causes of adult learning and to understand its timing. Through face-to-face interviews and telephone conversations with a national representative sample of almost 2,000 adult Americans 25 years of age and older, the authors asked adult learners to explain why they had gone back to school or decided to study on their own. The authors also asked them to list what topics they were studying, when, where, and how.

Americans in Transition contains the authors' findings regarding the causes and the timing of adult learning. An additional separate report will concentrate more fully on the topics, locations, schedules, and methods of adult learning.

Together the two works will constitute a major contribution to the literature in the field. They build on current scholarly investigations of the adult life cycle, relating stages in that cycle to adult learning. They offer an explanation of adult learning that should stimulate further research as well as guide current practices in adult learning. Indeed, they provide a projection of future directions for a learning society.

ACKNOWLEDGMENTS

We are grateful to the many people who assisted us in planning, conducting, and reporting this nationwide study of adult learning. As a major investigative effort to address the fundamental question, Why do adults learn?, we needed the good judgment and diligent assistance of many professionals in the field. The success of our study, both in producing information to explain adult learning and in drawing conclusions and implications to assist the profession as a whole, owes much to these individuals.

An advisory panel was assembled early in the course of the study to help us shape our objectives, identify our population, and develop an approach to gathering information from adults across the nation. The participation of the following people was important in this phase: Robert Calvert, Jr., Robert Glover, Ronald Gross, Richard Johnson, Francis Keppel, William N. Lovell, Francis U. Macy, Donald M. Reynolds, Charles Stalford, and Allen Tough. While these individuals represented interests of the federal government, cultural institutions, academic institutions, and the research community, we benefited additionally from the able assistance of College Board staff, including Solomon Arbeiter, Charles Bedford, Pamela Christoffel, Ronald Miller, and Donna M. Pokorny.

During the final stages of our work, we consulted with others who reviewed our findings and suggested ways to maximize their impact on professionals and practitioners in the field of adult learning as well as on the nation's adult population. We appreciate the help supplied by Martin A. Cory, Susan Davis, Gary Eyre, Ray Lewis, Richard Peterson, William G. Shannon, William C. Spann, and, once more, Robert Calvert, Jr., and Charles Stalford.

We would like to express special gratitude to K. Patricia Cross for reviewing the manuscript and sharing with us her useful suggestions and special insights. Her wisdom led to improvements in the clarity and quality of the text.

As authors of the study, we were supported by the able assistance and dedication of Marsha Davis Ullman, who served as research assistant during the entire investigation. The many hours she devoted to preparing the survey instruments, reviewing the mounds of computer printouts, and producing this final document were invaluable to us.

Furthermore, we acknowledge and appreciate the assistance of the Valley Forge Information Service, the group that conducted telephone interviews with our adults. In particular, we are grateful for the hard work and extreme interest shown in the study by Steve Friedman of that organization.

Most important, we thank the thousands of Americans across the country who gave hours of their time meeting with us and talking to us over the telephone. Their descriptions of what made them decide to learn something new and to choose how to learn when they did made this study possible. We hope our findings serve them and other adult learners now and in the future by producing a supportive climate for lifelong learning in America.

C. B. A.
H. M. B.

New York
August 1980

PART I: THE STUDY

In this study, we set out to find what causes adults to learn, thinking that the results could help many groups. While current *descriptions* of adult learning are adequate, current *explanations* are not. By taking into consideration the scholarly and popular literature describing adult life as divided into stages, as well as the available evidence on the rapid rate of social change, we established several hypotheses as to what causes adults to learn.

Then we interviewed a national representative sample of almost 2,000 Americans 25 years of age and older through face-to-face interviews and telephone conversations. Our questions probed for explanations as to the causes and timing of adult learning. We also investigated the procedures used by adults to meet their learning objectives.

1

WHAT CAUSES ADULTS TO LEARN?

What causes adults to learn? If we could answer that question, we could better predict which adults would study what topics in what numbers. We could better anticipate what kinds of institutions they would choose and what credentials they would want. We could better predict the times, places, and teaching methods they would prefer and the prices they would pay.

Such predictions would help five groups interested in adult learning: (1) those who provide adult learning; (2) those who supply information and counseling to adults; (3) those who make public policy for adult learning; (4) adults who are learning or who should be learning; and (5) scholars who study adult learning.

PROVIDERS. Two types of providers could benefit from reliable predictions about adult learning. They are those institutions and agencies whose primary function is education and those whose primary function falls in other areas—business, art, religion—but which also offer learning opportunities. Hence, providers include colleges and universities, professional and graduate schools, employers, museums, libraries, churches, civic organizations, the media, the military, publishers, and others.

INFORMATION AND COUNSELING CENTER STAFFS. There are roughly 25,000 centers in the United States that offer information and/or counseling to adults. These include special centers in colleges and universities, brokering centers, libraries, YMCA's and YWCA's, and private agencies, among others. As adults turn to learning in ever-increasing numbers, information and counseling centers that can assist them with educational planning will be in greater demand.

PUBLIC POLICYMAKERS. As lifelong learning becomes more prevalent, federal and state governments will become increasingly concerned about the supporting role they can play. The support could include financial as well as technical assistance with institutional programming, provision of information services, coordination of public resources, etc.

ADULTS. There are 126 million adults 25 years of age and older. Some are current learners and all are potential learners. If we could understand what makes some adults learn, we could offer advice to other adults about what, when, how, and where they might also want or need to learn. We could help them recognize opportunities or obligations to learn when they occur and we could help them anticipate the benefits of learning and the costs of not learning — or perhaps the reverse. In short, if we assume that learning is a constructive adult activity and if we can understand why some adults undertake it, we should be able to help other adults know whether they should do the same. Moreover, by displaying the entire range of adult learning, we might even be able to help the current learners see whole new possibilities for learning still more.

SCHOLARS. A small number of scholars have made adult learning their specialty. A larger number of investigators — some in college and university institutional research organizations — have examined adult learning. The number of studies has grown as adult education has expanded. What previous research has been able to do is to describe adult education and offer some explanations of it. That is, we know what, when, where, and how adults learn and we have some understanding of what causes them to learn. If we could gain further insights into the causes of adult learning, it would stimulate further research in this area.

But better predictions must wait for better answers to the question, "What causes adults to learn?" We need a deeper explanation, one that identifies at least the main streams in the adult learning movement and that helps us anticipate which way those streams will flow in coming years.

DESCRIPTIONS AND EXPLANATIONS OF ADULT LEARNING

To describe adult learning is one thing; to explain adult learning is another. That distinction is useful because descriptions and explanations have different purposes and because the available descriptions are more substantial than the available explanations.

Current Descriptions of Adult Learning

We have rather complete descriptions of adult learning at the present time. We know how many adults choose formal study in institutions rather than learning on their own. We know what kinds of institutions—two-year or four-year, public or private, educational or otherwise—adults attend. We know how many enroll full-time and how many enroll part-time, and whether they go to school days, nights, or weekends. We know what they study. We know whether they are studying for academic credit or not. We know whether they are seeking degrees or certificates. We know how many take examinations to demonstrate what they have learned rather than taking courses to learn it.

In addition, we know a great deal about the characteristics of adult learners and how they differ from nonlearners according to age, sex, marital status, race, education, occupation, income, and other demographic indicators.

There is, of course, more to learn. For example, no one knows how many adults participate in learning. The numerous studies have produced more disagreement than agreement. Depending on the definition of an adult, the definition of learning, and the method of conducting the study, estimates of adult learning range from 12 percent to 98 percent—a range far too wide to guide the development of an overarching explanation or to influence public policy decisions.

Features of Adult Learning Needing an Explanation

There are so many aspects of adult learning to be explained that the explanations are not as satisfactory as the descriptions. A fully satisfactory set of explanations would have to encompass at least these phenomena: the widespread participation of adults in learning, the unequal participation of adults, the rising rate of adult learning, and the fact that adults often do not learn what they say they will.

WIDESPREAD PARTICIPATION. All studies indicate that adult learning is commonplace. Even the lowest estimate of 12 percent—a conservative figure which counts only "organized instructions"—makes learning an activity engaging 19 million Americans. That is widespread participation by any standard; and virtually all other studies have produced a higher number.

Why is learning chosen as an activity by so many millions of adults?

UNEQUAL PARTICIPATION. The triennial surveys of adult participation prepared by the National Center for Education Statistics and the Bureau of the Census indicate that some groups are not engaged in adult learning in numbers comparable to their proportion of the national population. In an analysis of the 1969, 1972, and 1975 studies, Edward Cohen-Rosenthal found that blacks have not joined the ranks of adult learners in equal proportion to their rise in population. He also found that college-educated adults constituted only 25 percent of the population but more than 50 percent of the adult learners in 1975 (Cohen-Rosenthal, 1977).

K. Patricia Cross (1979) summarized the relationship of adult characteristics to adult learning as revealed in more than 30 major studies conducted in the past five years. Learning is more common among adults who are young, white, well-educated, rich, live in the West, reside in suburbs, and work longer hours. The best single correlate of learning among all of these adults is educational attainment.

Richard Anderson and Gordon Darkenwald (1979) studied adult dropouts and found that age, educational attainment, and race show a modest but consistent relationship with persistence in adult education. Adults who are younger, less educated, and black are more likely to drop out.

Why do these demographic characteristics correlate with adult learning?

RISING RATE. Apart from increased adult learning due to a growing adult population, a rising percentage of adults are seeking learning. Adult learners increased 21 percent from 1969 to 1972 while their numbers in the population increased only about 7 percent. Adult learners increased 8 percent between 1972 and 1975 while their numbers in the population increased only 5 percent.

Cross (1979), using roughly comparable data from 1957, suggested that the lowest estimate of 12 percent (for 1975) was only about 8 percent in 1957. It seems clear that the rate of adult participation in learning activities is rising over the long term, despite variations in the rate of rise from year to year.

Why are more and more adults taking part in learning activities?

UNRELIABLE DATA ON LEARNING PREFERENCES. There have been many studies of adults' interests in learning something in the future. A later look at how many adults actually learn usually shows a sharp drop in the number. Their expressed interest is not converted into action.

A typical example comes from the *Tenth Annual Gallup Poll of the Public's Attitudes Toward the Public Schools.* Gallup

(1978) asked 1,539 adults 18 years of age and older the following questions and got these answers:

Are you now taking, or have you ever taken, any courses in an adult education program?

Yes	31%
No	68%
Don't recall/	
no answer	1%

Would you be interested next year in taking any special courses or training in any fields or in any subjects?

Yes	41%
No	54%
Don't recall/	
no answer	5%

Clearly, if only 31 percent of the adults have *ever* enrolled in programs in all past years combined, the enrollment will not be 41 percent next year alone. This is the kind of discrepancy (which shows up in many such studies) between the number who express "interest" in learning and the number who actually learn.

Current Explanations of Adult Learning

We have a number of explanations of adult learning, some of them stretching back some 50 years. The explanations are successful to a greater or lesser degree in accounting for adult participation and persistence in learning. One reason for their mixed success in delineating the causes of adult learning and predicting what adults will do in the future is the complexity of what appear to be many forces determining adults' decisions to learn.

The Study of Complexities

Michael O'Keefe (1977) points out that there are "many problems in developing models with strong predictive powers." In presenting several estimates of future participation in adult education, O'Keefe warns his readers that "they present extrapolations of present trends rather than theory-based predictions of future behavior."

Cross, considering future demands for adult education, finds it difficult to predict because we have only weak explanations of why adults learn.

> As to our ability to construct "demand curves" and to predict the probable impact of various entitlement proposals on participation rates, I doubt that much accuracy can be achieved, given the rudimentary development of research on "voluntary" education. We need a great deal more understanding of the extent of slippage between market surveys and actual participation; and we need much more study of the motivational factors affecting adult participation in learning activities. (Cross 1978a, p. 15)

Commenting on our ability to develop an overarching theory of human behavior, Bernice Neugarten writes:

> One of our problems lies in the fact that we are as yet without sufficient systematic data on adults. A few sets of data have been reported in which individuals have been studied from childhood into adulthood . . . but these studies are few in number, and despite the growing recognition of the importance of longitudinal research, there have been as yet no major longitudinal studies of men and women as they move from youth to middle age, or from middle age to old age. There have been even fewer carefully designed and well-controlled cross-sectional studies of adult personality in which age differences, to say nothing of age *changes,* have constituted a central axis of investigation.
>
> Not only is there a paucity of data, but more important we are without a useful theory. Personality theorists have not for the most part faced the questions of stability and change over the entire life cycle. Attention has been focused primarily upon the first two but not on the last five sevenths of life. (Neugarten 1968, p. 137)

Because they have found demographic factors to have only limited explanatory power, Anderson and Darkenwald call for "more sophisticated conceptions":

> Sociodemographic variables such as age, sex, income, and schooling appear to play a relatively modest role in influencing the educational participation and persistence behavior of American adults. While variables such as age and schooling are of interest to policymakers because they identify groups that are po-

tential targets for educational intervention, they are of relatively modest importance if one wishes to explain and predict participation and persistence in adult education. Future research needs to employ more sophisticated conceptions of the participation process that include personal and situational variables (e.g., attitudes toward education, life change events such as marriage, job loss, and retirement, and awareness of adult education opportunities) that can reasonably be postulated to affect the nature and timing of engagement in further learning activities. (Anderson and Darkenwald 1979, pp. 5-6)

Some Explanations of Participation and Persistence

A number of scholars have made significant progress during the past 20 years in examining adult learning and analyzing its causes. They have offered explanations of why some adults initiate learning activities and why other adults do not; they have done the same for why some adults continue to learn and others do not. The explanations summarized here are among the most substantial in the field.

WHY ADULTS INITIATE LEARNING. Cyril Houle (1961) offers an analysis of adult motivations to learn. Three classes of adult learners emerge from his analysis: (1) the *goal-oriented* who learn to accomplish specific objectives; (2) the *activity-oriented* who learn to develop social contacts and relationships with others; and (3) the *learning-oriented* who learn for the sheer pleasure of acquiring knowledge for its own sake. While any single adult's reasons for learning may encompass all three classes, Houle points out that a central emphasis is usually discernible.

In attempting to explain why adults become motivated for any one or more of these three reasons, Houle points to several requirements: "the recognition of a need or interest, the will to do something about it, and the opportunity to do so." While acknowledging the importance of a need or interest—brought on by external events in one's life such as job promotions, deaths, or divorces—he places greater significance on "the internal process which makes the event when it occurs, crucial in changing the pattern of life" (Houle 1961, p. 57).

Finally, Houle proposes five factors that lead adults to lifelong learning: family background; teachers and schools; public libraries; occupation; and the exchange of friends. Lifelong learners, he claims, have had strong relationships with their parents, have had positive exchanges with previous teachers and schooling, have used public libraries as an important resource during their development, wanted to change their occupations, and were often stimulated by others to continue their learning.

Numerous factor analytic studies have been done, and most verify and expand Houle's classification. One such study by Barry Morstain and John Smart (1977) enhances our understanding of adult motivations to learn by identifying the following five distinct types of adult learners: (1) non-directed learners who have no specific goals; (2) social learners who want to improve their social interests and personal associations; (3) stimulation-seeking learners who learn to escape from routine and boredom; (4) career-oriented learners who learn because of occupational interests; and (5) life change learners who learn to improve multiple facets of their lives — career, intellectual, social, etc.

WHY SOME ADULTS CONTINUE TO LEARN. Cross has also examined the results of a large number of surveys which show that adults who continue learning are those who are already among the better educated. As a consequence, she offers three possible explanations:

> Broadly speaking there are three hypotheses for the consistent and positive relationship between educational attainment and educational interest. One is that education has done such a good job that the more people experience it the more they like it — either for its intrinsic or extrinsic rewards. A second hypothesis is that those who have been successful in the fairly narrow demands of the educational system stay in it longer and also wish to return to the scene of their earlier success. A third hypothesis is that human beings are basically curious and enjoy learning, but that the haves possess the information and wherewithal to pursue learning that interests them, whereas the have nots are handicapped and thwarted in attaining what all people basically desire. (Cross 1978a, p. 12)

In short, Cross suggests that "those with high motivation, high past success, good information networks, and adequate funds get more and more education while those already drag-

ging in the educational race fall farther and farther behind."
For this group, she explains, "The same things that led to relatively early school leaving undoubtedly contribute to lack of
interest in returning" (Cross 1978a).

WHY SOME ADULTS DO NOT INITIATE LEARNING. Cross has examined the results of a number of surveys which offered nonlearning adults a list of possible barriers and asked them to
check off the ones that were stopping them from learning. Her
analysis led her to classify such barriers into three groups:

- *Situational barriers* are those arising from one's situation in
  life at a given time, such as lack of time due to home or job
  responsibilities, lack of transportation, geographical isola-
  tion, lack of child care, etc.

- *Dispositional barriers* are those referring to attitudes about
  learning and perceptions of oneself as a learner. Feeling
  "too old" to learn, lack of confidence, and boredom with
  school are examples of dispositional barriers.

- *Institutional barriers* include those erected by learning institutions or agencies that exclude or discourage certain
  groups of learners because of such things as inconvenient
  schedules, full-time fees for part-time study, or restrictive
  locations.

Cross herself questions the reliability of the data on the
apparent barriers and calls for better information to show
"which barriers are real and which are simply convenient ra-
tionalizations." Her reservations seem well-founded. For example, the College Board has recently collected information
from 3,500 workers in a truck plant to find out why 99.5 percent do not use the tuition reimbursement plan that their
own union leaders negotiated into their current contract with
the manufacturer. The tuition reimbursement plan is a method
designed to remove economic barriers to learning by having
the company pay for any job-related training — training that
can include earning college degrees. The economic barriers
have been removed, but the workers themselves have not been
motivated to go to school, to take television or correspondence
courses, or even to undertake independent study. Evidently the

economic barriers were less real than rationalization (Brickell, 1979).

WHY SOME ADULTS DO NOT CONTINUE LEARNING. Anderson and Darkenwald analyzed an extensive body of data on the characteristics of adults who discontinued their learning, but found disappointingly weak relationships. They report:

> Despite a very large and representative sample and data on a large number of seemingly important variables, only 10 percent of the variance associated with participation and with persistence could be accounted for statistically. In other words, 90 percent of whatever it is that leads adults to participate in and drop out from adult education has not been identified by this or by other similar studies conducted in the past. (Anderson and Darkenwald 1979, p. 5)

The strongest relationships among a generally weak set indicated that younger adults are more likely to drop out of a learning situation than older adults; those with fewer years of schooling are more likely to drop out than those with more education; and those who are black are more likely not to continue education than others. Discontinuance, however, is an important phenomenon and it deserves a thorough explanation. It was the disappointing findings of this study that led Anderson and Darkenwald to call for "more sophisticated conceptions."

The Need for a Better Explanation

Despite the substantial contribution of these studies, our current understanding of adult learning needs to be even deeper if we are to predict what adults will do in the future, and to construct social policies to intervene in the natural course of events and make deliberate improvements. Otherwise, adult learning may continue to be primarily the domain of the well-educated and the well-off at a time when there is a strong public policy interest in encouraging other adults to learn as well.

3

SEARCHING FOR A BETTER EXPLANATION

We began our search for a better explanation of adult learning by turning to the near flood of current scholarly and popular literature dealing with the nature of adult life. We found that virtually all the literature on the subject divides adult life into stages. Depending on the disciplines in which they were trained, different writers see the life stages as phases in the biological, psychological, or social dimensions of life. Accordingly, they see the movement from one stage to another as necessitating biological, psychological, or social adaptations; and they see these adaptations as requiring adults to adjust and grow.

Current Literature on the Adult Life Cycle

In this chapter, we provide a sampling of the literature currently available on the adult life cycle.

Daniel Levinson, in *The Seasons of a Man's Life*, describes "the great hidden pattern that underlies and shapes every man's life" and points out how "human beings continue to change throughout their lifetimes according to an age-linked timetable." He identifies four overlapping developmental pe-

Figure 1: THE SEASONS OF A MAN'S LIFE

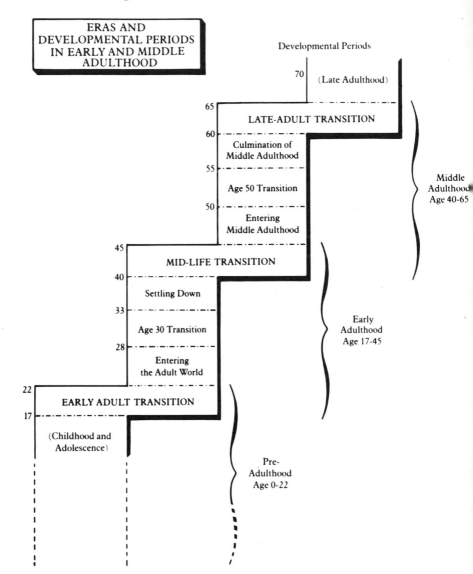

SOURCE: Adapted from Daniel J. Levinson, *The Seasons of a Man's Life.*
Copyright © 1978 by Daniel J. Levinson. Reprinted by permission of Alfred
A. Knopf, Inc.

riods in the adult life cycle, each lasting some 25 years, punctuated or separated by five transitions (Figure 1). Unlike the developmental periods, each transition occurs during a relatively short age span.

Levinson found that man traverses the periods in a given order and must deal with the developmental tasks appropriate to each stage. Moreover, he points out that there is a "relatively low variability in the age at which each period begins and ends." According to Levinson, each developmental period is distinguished by its own life style, which has biological, psychological, and social aspects. He concludes that no period is inherently better than the others:

> Again, the imagery of the seasons is useful. Spring is not intrinsically a better season than winter, nor is summer better than spring. (Levinson 1978, p. 319)

Roger Gould, in *Transformations: Growth and Change in Adult Life,* writes about growth as the obligation and opportunity of adulthood. Growth is necessary to cope with a predictable sequence of changing patterns and preoccupations during the adult years.

> ... *adulthood is not a plateau;* rather it is a dynamic and changing time for all of us. As we grow and change, we take steps *away* from childhood and *toward* adulthood — steps such as marriage, work, consciously developing a talent or buying a home. With each step, the unfinished business of childhood intrudes, disturbing our emotions and requiring psychological work. With this in mind, adults may now view their disturbed feelings at particular periods as a possible sign of progress, as part of their attempted movement toward a fuller adult life. (Gould 1978, p. 14)

Gould found that most problems of adulthood are age related and that adults take a characteristic view during each era.

> At the end of our twenties, with our place in the world somewhat secure, we could afford to rediscover vital talents and instincts we had been suppressing; we could consider amending our life course to include them. During our early thirties, we acted tentatively to make some changes and fussed and fretted about the rest. . . . [In our forties] we see more clearly, and consequently are more frightened. For we know that we must act on

our new vision of ourselves and the world. The desire for stability and continuity which characterized our thirties is being replaced by a relentless inner demand for action. The sense of timelessness in our early thirties is giving away to an awareness of the pressure of time in our forties. (Gould 1978, p. 217)

In addition, Gould, like other investigators, saw the significance of specific events as milestones along the adult life course.

Certain key events — buying a first house, a first car, experiencing a first job, a first baby, the first loss of a parent, first physical injury or first clear sign of aging — force us to see ourselves more as the creators of our lives and less as living out the lives we thought were our destiny. (Gould 1978, p. 13)

Lowenthal, Thurnher, and Chiriboga, in *Four Stages of Life* (1975), identified four stages in the adult years: (1) early adulthood, (2) parenthood, (3) post-parenthood, and (4) retirement. They then studied four separate groups of women and men in "pretransitional" periods just before moving into the four stages to find out how they prepared for them. They examined high school seniors, young newlyweds, middle-aged parents with grown children, and a group about to retire. Highlights of their findings include the following:

- *Impending transitions are stressful:* ". . . all such changes, whether incremental (involving role gain) or decremental (involving role loss), are potentially stressful." (p. x)

- *They often cause a personal reassessment:* "The anticipation of an impending transition often serves as a stimulus to examine, and possibly to reorient, goals and aspirations, and to reassess personal resources and impediments in the light of the probability of their attainment." (p. x)

- *Work-related events are especially stressful for the middle-aged:* "Work-related problems were critical for the middle-aged men, mainly having to do with lack of advancement and the pressures of assuring sufficient income to maintain a comfortable life style throughout the retirement period." (pp. 229-230)

- *The young experience a larger number of stressful events than the old, partly because the young engage in a broader span of activities:* "The number of life-course events, or stressors, reported over the prior year *declined* across successive stages in the adult life course, with a sharp drop between newlyweds and the middle-aged but only slight differences between the middle-aged and the preretirement groups." (p. 229)

- *Women experience more stressful events than men. Differences among the sexes were far more significant than differences between the youngest and the oldest of each sex viewed separately:* "Women in all stages reported more stressful experiences than men." (p. 229)

In addition to what the authors regard as the major transitions between the four life stages, they also found what they call idiosyncratic transitions within the stages — geographic moves, divorce, illness or injury of the adult, illness or injury of a loved one, sojourns in another culture, and the loss of a loved one through death — that have a profound bearing on adult adaptation, nonadaptation, or maladaptation. Many adults reported considerable change in their values, feelings, and behavior patterns accompanying or following such events.

George Vaillant, in *Adaptation to Life,* reports the results of a 40-year longitudinal study of almost 300 Harvard graduates (known as the Grant Study) and evidence to support earlier formulations by Erik Erikson.

> The evidence from the Grant Study confirms the adult life patterns outlined by Erik Erikson in *Childhood and Society.* . . . [Erikson] was among the first social scientists to appreciate fully that adults do not march on from life event to life event, from graduation to marriage to "empty nest" to retirement. Instead, he demonstrated that adults change dynamically in the process. (Vaillant 1977, p. 201)

The longitudinal look at adult life patterns persuaded Vaillant that "There *are* patterns and rhythms to the life cycle." Moreover, Vaillant's analysis

> . . . supported Erikson's hypothesis that the stages of the life cycle must be passed through in sequence. Although one stage of life is not superior to another, a given stage of development could rarely be achieved until the previous one was mastered. (1977, p. 207)

As evidence to support the stability of life cycles, Vaillant points out that

> . . . isolated traumatic events rarely mold individual lives. That is not to say that the premature death of a parent, the unexpected award of a scholarship, the chance first encounter with a future spouse, or a heart attack will not result in a sudden change in life's trajectory. . . . But the quality of the whole journey is seldom changed by a single turning. (1977, p. 368)

Still, Vaillant found that the lives of the Harvard men did not unfold with clocklike precision.

> The life cycle is more than an invariant sequence of stages with single predictable outcomes. . . . If we follow adults for years, we can uncover startling changes and evolutions. We can discover developmental discontinuities in adults that are as great as the difference in personality between a 9-year-old and what he becomes at 15. (Vaillant 1977, pp. 372-373)

Thus Vaillant's findings confirm the idea of a life pattern unfolding in a sequence punctuated by critical events.

Gail Sheehy, in *Passages: Predictable Crises of Adult Life,* reports her interviews with 115 people whom she describes as a "pacesetter group—healthy, motivated people who either began in or entered the middle class, though some began in poverty, even ghettos." The people ranged in age from 18 to 55 years and included high-achieving women as well as high-achieving men.

Sheehy's case studies led her to conclude that "life after adolescence is *not* one long plateau," a conclusion she said had been reached earlier by William Shakespeare, Else Frenkel-Brunswik, Erik Erikson, Margaret Mead, Daniel Levinson, Roger Gould, and others. Sheehy echoed Gould in pointing out that "times of crisis, of disruption or constructive change, are not only predictable but desirable. They mean growth."

Sheehy identified a standard series of life stages which she calls "Pulling Up Roots," "The Trying Twenties," "Catch-30," "Rooting and Extending," "The Deadline Decade," and "Renewal or Resignation." In order to avoid the use of the word *crisis*, because it implied personal failure, weakness, or an inability to bear up against stressful outside events, Sheehy "replaced that confusing label with a less loaded word for the critical transitions between stages and called them *passages*." She found that the transitions were often difficult.

> The work of adult life is not easy. As in childhood, each step presents not only new tasks of development but requires a letting go of the techniques that worked before. With each passage some magic must be given up, some cherished illusion of safety and comfortably familiar sense of self must be cast off, to allow for the greater expansion of our own distinctiveness. (Sheehy 1976, p. 31)

But she points out that the challenge of a transition is the opportunity for growth.

> It would be surprising if we didn't experience some pain as we leave the familiarity of one adult stage for the uncertainty of the next. But the willingness to move through each passage is equivalent to the willingness to live abundantly. If we don't change, we don't grow. If we don't grow, we are not really living. Growth demands a temporary surrender of security. (Sheehy 1976, p. 513)

Sheehy, too, found adult life to be punctuated by critical events. "Everything that happens to us — graduations, marriage, childbirth, divorce, getting or losing a job — affects us. These *marker events* are the concrete happenings of our lives." (Marker event is the term used by Daniel Levinson to define a particular occasion or extended period that brings about or signifies a notable change in the person's life, though a marker event is not always present to signal change.) But, like other writers, Sheehy points out that the marker events are not as important as the life stages.

> A developmental stage, however, is not defined in terms of marker events; it is defined by changes that begin within. The underlying impulse toward change will be there regardless of whether or not it is manifested in or accentuated by a marker event. . . . The inner realm is where the crucial shifts in bedrock begin to throw a person off balance, signaling the necessity to change and move on to a new footing in the next stage of development. (Sheehy 1976, pp. 29-30)

Sheehy emphasizes the importance of internal changes — biological and psychological — in determining life stages and the transitions between them. Not all authors agree. Bernice Neugarten, in *Middle Age and Aging,* claims that the biological model of explaining personality change in the adult years is insufficient:

> . . . we need a social framework for understanding the timing patterns that occur. . . . There is a prescriptive timetable for the ordering of life events: a time when men and women are expected to marry, a time to raise children, a time to retire. (Neugarten 1968, pp. 142-143)

Neugarten points out that this pattern is adhered to, more or less consistently, by most persons in this society. By way of explanation, she writes:

> Age norms and age expectations operate as prods and brakes upon behavior, in some instances hastening an event, in others, delaying it. Men and women are not only aware of the social clocks that operate in various areas of their lives, but they are also aware of their own timing and readily describe themselves as "early," or "late," or "on time" with regard to family and occupational events. . . . The saliency of age and age-norms in influencing the behavior of adults is no less than in influencing the behavior of children. (1968, pp. 143-144)

Empirical studies demonstrating the importance of social influences on establishing adult life stages, she continues

> . . . have relevance for a theory of the psychology of the life-cycle in two ways: First, in indicating that the age structure of a society, the internalization of age-norms, and age-group identifications are important dimensions of the social and cultural context in which the course of the individual life line must be viewed; second, because these concepts point to at least one additional way of structuring the passage of time in the life span of the individual, *providing a time clock* that can be superimposed over the biological clock, together they help us to comprehend the life cycle.

> The major punctuation marks in the adult life line tend (those, that is, which are orderly and sequential) to be more often social than biological — or, if biologically based, they are often biological events that occur to significant others rather than to oneself, like grandparenthood or widowhood. If psychologists are to discover order in the events of adulthood, and if they are to discover order in the personality changes that occur in all individ-

uals as they age, we should look to the social as well as the biological clock, and certainly to social definitions of age and age-appropriate behavior. (Neugarten 1968, p. 146)

Neugarten also took into account specific life events, but, like other investigators, found them less important than the inevitable life stages. Thus, Neugarten identified life events as well as life stages and found the stages set by a biological/social clock.

Nancy Schlossberg, in *A Model for Analyzing Human Adaptation to Transition,* also notes the rising interest in the idea of adulthood as a time of change "not only from theorists and researchers in the social sciences but also from practitioners in the helping professions, from the mass media, and from the general public."

The problems connected with aging, the plight of the elderly, the panic of the middle-aged are the subjects of numerous popular books and articles. Such terms as *transition, crisis, adaptation, coping,* and *stress* have become key points of discussion. (Schlossberg 1979, p. 1)

Schlossberg herself uses the term *transition* broadly

. . . to include not only obvious life changes such as high school graduation, job entry, marriage, birth of the first child, and bereavement, but also such subtle factors as the loss of one's career aspirations and even the non-occurrence of anticipated events (e.g., an expected job promotion that never comes through). (Schlossberg 1979, p. 6)

Schlossberg distinguishes between successful and unsuccessful transitions. She found three sets of factors that affect how one adapts to a transition and influence the outcome: first were the characteristics of the transition itself such as role change, source, timing, onset, duration, affect, and degree of stress; second were the characteristics of the pretransition and posttransition environments, such as interpersonal support systems, institutional supports, and the physical environment; and third were the characteristics of the individual going through the transition, such as sex, age, state of health, race, ethnic background, socioeconomic status, value orientation, psychosocial competence, and previous experience with a transition of a similar nature.

Alan Knox, in *Adult Development and Learning,* examines

the life events discussed by Schlossberg, Neugarten, Sheehy, Lowenthal, and others and joins them in pointing out that such events bring about role changes requiring adaptations.

> The relative stability of adult life is periodically punctuated by change events such as marriage, a job change, or the death of a close friend, that alter significantly the individual's relationships with other people and disturb the routine of social participation. . . . These events may occur in any relationship—family, occupational, or community. They may entail a gain, a loss, or a combination of gains and losses in role relationships. . . . Because change events entail alterations in role relationships, some adaptation is inescapable. (Knox 1977, pp. 513-514, 548)

Knox also sees adult life divided into segments or stages and adult concerns shifting as adults move from one stage to another. In early adulthood, the most significant change events are related to the worker role. Those events include starting a new job, changing jobs, moving to a new community for a new job, and losing a job. During the middle part of adulthood, events tend to be related to family roles such as seeing grown children leave for college, begin work, or marry; going through divorce and remarriage; or simply shifting attention from work to home. In later adulthood, a change in the adult role as worker again becomes prominent as adults move toward and into retirement. (The pattern described here is particularly true for men.)

While he admits that there has been "little systematic study of the adaptation strategies that adults use to adjust to change events," Knox proposes that there are at least six ways adults adapt to significant change events: frantic activity, action, educative activity, seeking assistance, contemplation, and withdrawal. We were most intrigued by Knox's attention to educative activity as one way adults deal with changes.

> When a change event occurs, the need for some adaptation produces, for some adults at least, a heightened readiness to engage in educative activity. The resulting educative activity may be directly or indirectly related to the change event, and the relation may or may not be recognized by the individual. . . . The educative activity may include all types of informal information seeking such as reading or talking with others, as well as more formal participation in part-time, externally sponsored educa-

tional programs. Familiar instances of increased educative activity related to change events occur in relation to the birth of the first child, the purchase of a new car, or major job change. (Knox 1977, p. 539)

Of all the literature we read, Knox went furthest in linking adult learning to adult life changes.

From the Literature: Some Central Ideas About Adult Life

The major ideas about adulthood that emerge from the literature fall into a rather clear pattern, even though some authors stress one idea and some another, and not all agree on every idea. The main lines of their writing are summarized briefly here.

The course of adult life is divided into stages through which adults move in a fixed order and at relatively fixed times. The stages are rooted in the biological, psychological, and social nature of adult human beings and constitute the major demarcations in the human life cycle. Passing from one stage to another constitutes a significant transition. Adults lose equilibrium in an earlier stage and must regain it in a later one. Thus, transitions pose challenges, create stress, and offer opportunities for growth. Adults cope in different ways with their life transitions and enjoy different degrees of success, depending partly on their personal characteristics and partly on their situation.

While the authors disagree about their relative importance, they recognize the existence of biological and psychological events that are *internal* to the adult as well as social and economic events that are *external*. These specific life events, whether internal or external, often signal the beginning or end of a life stage, although significant events occur within as well as between stages. Most authors see the events as having a precipitating rather than a causative effect. That is, they often release a latent stream of activity driven by forces that have already built up a potential for action. On the other hand, major events that do not occur on schedule or that have a traumatic effect—what Sheehy calls *untimely events* and *life accidents*—can be sufficiently powerful to deflect adults from the patterned movement from one life stage to another.

What interested us most in these formulations was that transitions challenge adults and require them to grow. Could this be the better explanation of adult learning we were seeking?

On the assumption that transitions in adult life are influenced by social and economic change — and, to some extent, precipitate still more social and economic change — we turned our attention to the current literature on social change. We found that adult life has become more turbulent and can be expected to become even more so in future years.

Rapid Social Change[1]

It was clear even to the casual observer that the growth in adult learning was taking place during a period of rapid social change. Admittedly, American life is in a virtually continuous state of rapid social change. Every decade since 1900, as well as many of those before, could be described as a 10-year period of rapid social change. The 1960s and 1970s were certainly not exceptions; and, as the 1970s ended, the 1980s and the 1990s promised more of the same. The nation can expect changes in its population, in the roles of women and minorities, in work, in economics, in family life, and in leisure.

POPULATION. The population has aged, shifting from a median age of 28 in 1970 to 30 in 1977, and it will continue to age. The 1980s will witness society's move from being young to middle-age. Four-fifths of the predicted growth will be among those people in their 30s and 40s, with the remainder in the 60-and-older group. One out of every eight Americans will be over 65 in the 1980s. Life expectancy will continue its steady rise: half of the children born in 1980 will reach the age of 73 and live beyond it. By 1990, the median age of the population will be over 34 years; by the year 2000, it will be over 37.

The nation's adults, already among the world's best educated, will continue to accumulate more years of schooling. By 1985, more than three out of four persons in the civilian

---

1. Most of the statistics cited in this section were taken from Guzzard (1979); Johansen (1977); and *U.S. News and World Report* (1979). See References for complete citations.

labor force will be high school graduates, and one out of five will have completed four or more years of college.

Restless Americans will continue to move at the rate of more than 20 percent a year — 10 percent within their current cities and 10 percent to new cities. The Sun Belt will continue to soak up the population of the Snow Belt, drawing people away from the declining cities of the Northeast and the farmlands of the Midwest. More people will avoid big cities, choosing instead to live in small towns, villages, and even rural areas. Only 23 percent of Americans will be living in the cities by 1990 as compared with 27 percent today.

Small waves of immigrants will continue to arrive on American shores. About 375,000 immigrants have entered the country yearly since 1968, accounting for approximately 20 percent of population growth. A half-million newcomers will arrive every year, keeping the ranks of legal registered aliens above one million and the ranks of illegal aliens somewhere between 4 and 12 million — no one can be sure how many there will be.

WOMEN. The women's movement will continue to progress. Its success will be most convincingly expressed by the rising number of women in paid employment. During the period 1960 to 1978, the labor force drew more than 19 million women into its ranks, making up about 60 percent of its growth. In 1978 alone, the nation added three million new jobs; 66 percent of those new jobs went to women. Women already made up almost half of the labor force and over half of all women of working age were in part-time or full-time paid employment or were looking for work. Their numbers will grow steadily throughout the 1980s and beyond.

There were at least three powerful forces bringing women into the work place. One was economic pressures on families, necessitating a second income. About half of all households headed by married couples have both husband and wife working. A second was the spreading expectation that women should do more than maintain a home, especially after their children went off to school. Finally, there was the increased desire on the part of many women to lead active, productive lives in the economic mainstream and this was particularly true for the growing numbers of better-educated women.

Working mothers will become even more commonplace in the future. Of the women 25 to 34 years of age who entered the work force in 1978, more than 70 percent were mothers with dependent children, despite the problems of combining a job with family responsibilities. A balanced life for a married woman — with or without children — will come to be thought of as a combination of a home life and a working life. Most women will work for pay, but some will engage in volunteer work as a substitute.

In addition to their increasing role in the nation's economic life, women will be a growing force in politics, partly as voters and partly as elected officials. They will play an ever-stronger role in shaping public policy, adding further momentum to the women's movement.

MINORITIES. Racial and ethnic minorities will continue to rise in numbers. Blacks, now totaling 26 million or 11.8 percent of the population of the United States, will increase to 30 million or 12.2 percent by 1990. Hispanics, the nation's fastest growing minority, now total more than 12 million or 6 percent of the population. Last year alone there was a nationwide gain of one million Hispanics. Minorities will also increase their incomes, their education, and their political power. They will get better choices of jobs and better choices of places to live.

Nevertheless, the gap between the minorities and the majority will still exist. Those concerned with public policy will continue to intervene, as they did throughout the 1960s and the 1970s, in an attempt to close the gap or at least narrow it.

WORK. More than two million people on the average joined the labor force annually from 1968 to 1978, a growth of 28 percent. The labor force will continue its remarkably steady expansion, rising to 113 million paid workers by 1990 — up 11 percent from the 102 million at work in the final year of the 1970s, a short decade before.

There will be still more part-time workers which already number about 17 million. They were and will continue to be the fastest-growing segment of the labor force.

Technological change and the proliferation of government

regulation will continue to make work physically easier, but mentally harder, contributing to a continuing shift in the occupational mix, with a steadily rising proportion of professionals, managers, and service workers and a steadily declining fraction of laborers, machine operators, and craftspersons. Workers will be better off than before, working shorter hours for more pay, getting their benefits in the form of more leisure, more fringe benefits, and more cash. Their decisions about retirement will seesaw between a desire to start the good life as soon as possible and the fear that their retirement incomes will not be enough to pay for the good life. No one can be sure what the net effect on retirement decisions will be, but public policy will provide an increasing number of incentives to delay retirement and relieve the pressure on publicly funded pension systems.

ECONOMICS. Inflation, already at record highs throughout the 1970s, will continue to shrink pay checks, pension checks, and savings accounts. The economic squeeze will tighten, partly because of a slower rate of growth in worker productivity —from an annual rate of about 2 percent in the 1960s and earlier down to about 1 percent in the 1970s—and partly because of the redistribution of wealth to Third World countries through the rising prices they charge for oil and other raw materials.

Taxpayers will continue to resist the expansion of public services, partly because of economic stringencies in their personal budgets and partly because of disenchantment with the visionary social programs of the 1960s and 1970s.

FAMILY LIFE. Families, already at their smallest since the nation was founded, will shrink even further. At the end of the 1970s, more than half of the households in America were made up of only one or two persons; the average for all households was less than three. A rapid increase in "nonfamily households" also dominates the scene: single-member households are now 25 percent of the total, a 60 percent increase in the past eight years.

Adults will start having children later and stop having them earlier, partly because of the increasing number of women who want to work as long as possible before having children and who want to return to work as soon as possible after having them. The smaller number of children will mean less necessity for public service programs for the young — such as elementary and secondary education, and youth programs — just as the increasing age of the population will create a need for more public services for the elderly.

The rate of divorce and separation will continue to rise steadily, creating more single-parent homes and more single-person households. The number of divorced adults increased from two million in 1955 to eight million in 1977. Their proportion in the total population doubled from 2.6 percent in 1955 to 5 percent in 1976. Census experts have estimated that nearly one-half of all children born today will spend a "meaningful" portion of their childhood with only one parent.

The number of unmarried couples living together more than doubled in the first eight years of the 1970s. Their separations go unrecorded in the legal records, which thus understates the actual number of family dissolutions. But those unrecorded separations nevertheless increase the amount of emotional trauma that adults experience as they try to create satisfactory lifetime relationships. The same search shows up in the form of serial marriages, with divorce being followed by another marriage.

There were nearly 11 million widows in 1976, up one million since 1970. Women will continue to outlive men in the 1980s and 1990s, thereby increasing the number of widows.

LEISURE. Americans will have more leisure time, often choosing it in preference to longer working hours and higher incomes. They will put part of their leisure time into recreation, part into education, and part into unpaid volunteer work.

The size of the volunteer work force will continue its steady rise. More than 35 million adults were engaged in some form of volunteer work in the mid-1970s. The number will be higher in the 1980s, rising to 65 million in the final decade of the century. One reason among many will be cash-hungry government agencies turning to volunteers to help maintain their customary level of services without raising taxes to offset inflation.

Arriving at the Transitions Hypothesis

The outpouring of recent professional and popular literature made it evident that adult life—especially adult life in the United States—is filled with transitions. The transitions of younger people moving through infancy, childhood, and adolescence are followed by the transitions of older people moving through college, military service, marriage, employment, parenthood, church membership, union membership, civic or community leadership, home rental or ownership, relocation, retirement, loss of family and friends through death, personal infirmity, and finally death itself. Adulthood is not a time of stagnation or stability, at least in the early and middle years; instead it is a time of change.

Further, the information available on current and prospective social and economic changes made it apparent that more adults will experience life transitions in the future. Changes in population, mobility, technology, occupations, housing, income, inflation, government, family life, politics, minority affairs, and leisure will mean an even faster rate of change in adult life than ever before.

Forty Million Americans in Career Transition

During an earlier study probing career changes for adults, we found that the life area of paid employment is one of highly significant transitions for many adults. Those transitions included entry, progression, and exit not only with respect to specific jobs, but even with respect to career fields. We concluded from the study that some 40 million adults in the United States anticipated making a job or career change.

While conducting the study, we also investigated adult interest in learning as a means of making a successful job or career change. When we encountered adults who expressed an interest in changing their jobs or careers, we asked whether they thought they would need to learn anything to make the change; whether they wanted any information or advice about making the change or about further learning; how, when, and where they wanted that information or advice delivered; and what they would pay for it.

We were impressed with the high proportion—about 60

percent—who felt they would have to learn something in order to make a transition to a new job or career, even though not all of the 60 percent sought information or advice about what, when, or where to learn. In fact, many of the adults with whom we talked were already learning and on the way to making a change (Arbeiter et al., 1976).

One Hundred and Twenty-Six Million Americans in Life Transition

Later, as we examined the literature on the variety of life transitions experienced by adults, and the available information on social and economic trends, we began to realize that all adults —the 126 million who are 25 years of age and older—are in transition continually throughout their lives. If career transitions led many adults to learn, why not other life transitions? To make changes in areas other than paid employment might also require adults to learn something new.

Life Transitions as Reasons for Learning

Pursuing the previously discussed line of thinking led us to elaborate on the idea that adult life transitions might be reasons for adult learning. As a result, we formulated the following general proposition:

- *Moving from one status in life to another requires the learning of new knowledge, new skills, and/or new attitudes or values.* Becoming a foreman or a coach or an executive or a lieutenant requires new interpersonal relationships as well as new technical knowledge or skills. So does becoming a wife or a mother or a widow. So does joining a political party or a civic group or a service club or fraternal organization. It is the same with becoming a member of a church or civil rights group or attending a concert series or taking up bowling or dancing or tennis. All of them require learning.

The learning can be self-directed or it can be other-directed. That is, learning can be acquired informally through unstructured daily experience, or through informal but self-planned study, or through formal instruction designed and conducted by others. The important thing is not the method

Figure 2: DEFINITION OF TRANSITION

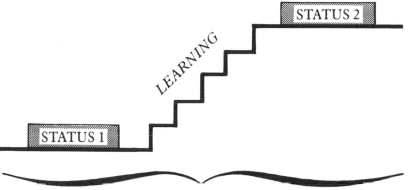

used, but that the learning takes place. If the learning is not accomplished, the adult cannot make a transition into the new status. The proposition is shown in Figure 2.

This definition of a transition allows for life changes smaller and less significant than those cataloged by Erickson, Neugarten, Sheehy, and others. But our proposition applies to all types of transitions. Transitions require learning: a little transition, a little learning; a large transition, a large amount of learning. Also, our definition seems more useful for understanding and predicting adult learning. For example, three weeks of learning is enough for an adult to make a transition from ordinary cook to gourmet cook; but three years of learning is necessary for an adult to make a transition from ordinary college graduate to licensed attorney. A job change can be a transition significant enough to require learning (see Figure 3).

The proposition, however, does not explain why adults make a status change at a particular point in time. Why not earlier? Why not later? After all, the learning opportunities are there every single day, but adults do not take advantage of them every day. How do adults schedule their transitions and thus their learning? Do they actually control their own schedules; or are they running on a biological, psychological, social, or economic timetable not under their control?

We knew from experience that all adults are surrounded by examples of what can be accomplished by learning. Their lives

Figure 3: EXAMPLE OF A TRANSITION

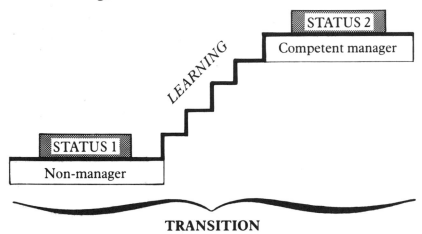

TRANSITION

are filled with teachers, business executives, professionals, government officials, union leaders, entertainers, relatives, friends, and acquaintances who have learned their way to success. We knew that some adults regret the learning opportunities they have let slip by and wish, hope, or believe that they will take advantage of them the next time. We suspected that other adults, using whatever information they have available, at least weigh the costs and benefits of future learning. But what makes them act?

Life Events as Triggers for Learning

What about the "marker events" Levinson discusses or the "stressors" Lowenthal talks about—the life events that signal a notable transition in an adult's life? Are there potential adult learners who will not learn unless there is some marker event triggering a latent desire to learn? Perhaps being ready, willing, and able to learn are not quite enough. Perhaps there also has to be an occurrence—a specific life event—serving as a starter's pistol to signal that the time has come to start learning in order to move on. The alternative to moving on when the event occurs is staying where you are.

We were intrigued with the notion that there are potential

Figure 4: DEFINITION OF TRIGGER

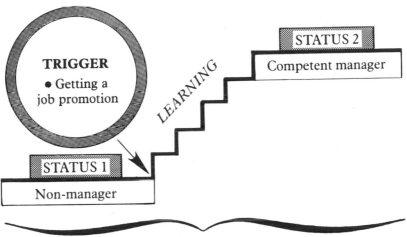

adult learners who plan, want, or need to learn, but who will not learn unless there are specific events in their lives to trigger their decisions to begin learning at a particular point in time. The idea of latent learners seemed rather natural. After all, if there is a trigger, there must be a bullet in the breech.

This thinking led us to formulate a second general proposition:

• *Some identifiable event triggers an adult's decision to learn at a particular point in time.* The need and the opportunity and even the desire are necessary but not sufficient. Something must happen to convert a latent learner into an active learner. The effect of the event is to cause the adult to begin learning at that point in time rather than at an earlier or later point. The second proposition has been added to Figure 4.

The Difference Between Transitions and Triggers

We thought hard about the distinction between life transitions and life triggers — whether it was a distinction worth making, and whether it could be made clearly. The following discus-

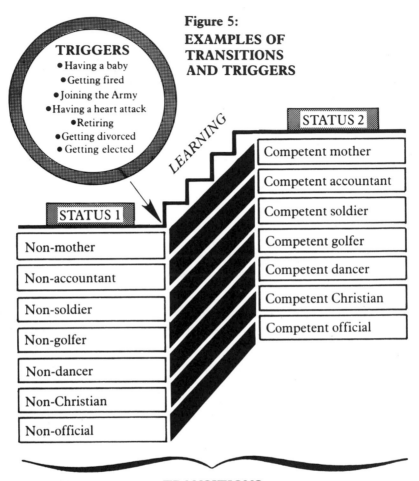

TRIGGERS
- Having a baby
- Getting fired
- Joining the Army
- Having a heart attack
- Retiring
- Getting divorced
- Getting elected

Figure 5:
EXAMPLES OF
TRANSITIONS
AND TRIGGERS

LEARNING

STATUS 2

Competent mother

Competent accountant

Competent soldier

Competent golfer

Competent dancer

Competent Christian

Competent official

STATUS 1

Non-mother

Non-accountant

Non-soldier

Non-golfer

Non-dancer

Non-Christian

Non-official

TRANSITIONS

sion reflects our thinking, reviewed and polished in light of the actual findings.

TRANSITIONS AS REASONS FOR LEARNING. The adult sees some benefit to be gained by moving from one status to another; the purpose of the learning is to gain that benefit. The transition is the change in status—past, present, or future—that makes learning necessary. The adult needs to become competent at something he or she could not do before in order to succeed in the new status. Thus the topic of learning is always related to the transition. For example, a person who studies accounting is making a transition into being an accountant, or if already an accountant, perhaps to being a certified accountant.

TRIGGERS AS TIMES FOR LEARNING. Something happens in the adult's life to precipitate the decision to learn at that point in time. If that event had occurred earlier or later, the learning would have been triggered earlier or later. Furthermore, the trigger may or may not be connected to the transition. Thus the topic of learning may not be related to the triggering event. For example, a person who is studying accounting may be a traveling salesperson who has suffered a heart attack.

Some illustrative transitions and triggers are shown in Figure 5. There may not be a one-to-one correspondence between the two.

LIFE AREAS FOR TRANSITIONS AND TRIGGERS. Philosophers and poets have been mapping life areas for thousands of years, and sociologists and psychologists have been mapping them for dozens of years. Man is biological and psychological, visceral and cerebral. Man has relationships with himself, with his family, with the larger community of man, and with God. There is work and there is leisure; there is family life and there is community life; there is religion; there is art, and there is health, both physical and mental.

We hypothesized that if life transitions were times of learning and that if specific events triggered the decisions to learn at particular points in time, then both the transitions and the triggers would occur in the several identifiable life areas. We thought it worthwhile to classify the transitions and the triggers — separately, in case they did not occur in the same arenas of life — into the following life areas: *Career, Family, Health, Religion, Citizenship, Art,* and *Leisure.*

We were uncertain how the transitions and triggers would be distributed into the seven categories, but we hypothesized that some would fall into each one.

PART II: FINDINGS

The findings, presented in the following chapters, provide evidence on what causes adults to learn, along with data on what and where they learn. Learners are contrasted with nonlearners according to their demographic characteristics.

The hypotheses established to guide the study are tested with the information collected during the interviews. The significance of moving from one stage in life to another as a cause of learning is analyzed, along with the pivotal role played by specific events that punctuate the life course.

4

INCIDENCE OF ADULT LEARNING

Half of all Americans 25 years and older (over 60 million adults) learned one or more topics in the past year according to our findings. This is remarkable evidence that we have indeed become a learning society (see Figure 6).

Definition of Learning

The 50 percent rate of participation in learning was revealed in answers to the question:

> There are many types of adult learning. It could be formal or informal, something you are teaching yourself—such as home maintenance, gardening, bowling, insurance, religion, child care—or it could be private lessons in music or art or dancing, or it could be adult education classes, or college courses, or training at your company. Anything at all. Are you studying or learning anything now or have you in the last 12 months?

> [If the respondent said "No" or expressed uncertainty, the following question was asked.] Are you sure that you are not studying or learning anything now or that you have not studied or learned anything in the last 12 months—taught yourself anything—watched a television course, joined a study group at

Figure 6: LEARNING NOW OR IN THE PAST 12 MONTHS

Applying these percentages to the 126 million Americans 25 years of age and older, this study indicates a population of 62 million adult learners. (Also appears as Table 1 in Appendix A.)

church or synagogue, learned tennis, taught yourself cooking or sewing, car repair, been in seminars or in training courses for your job, or taken any kinds of lessons?

The 50 percent participation rate exceeds that found in most earlier studies, but the differences can be explained.

Earlier Studies of Adult Participation Rates

The 1975 study made by the National Center for Education Statistics, using 1975 U.S. Bureau of the Census data gathered through its Current Population Survey, shows the rate of adult participation in learning at just under 12 percent. However, if this figure is adjusted upward to include all forms of independent learning in addition to the "organized instruction" counted by the Census; adjusted upward to include the full-time students excluded by the Census; adjusted upward to reflect the annual rate of increase in participation (an estimated 2 percent per year between 1975 and 1979); adjusted upward to accommodate the higher participation rate among the higher-income, better-educated, more managerial and professional respondents to the College Board survey; and adjusted downward to reflect the difference between the Census age group of 17 years and older and the College Board group of 25 years and older, the figures for participation rates would probably converge.

Taking a different example, the Carp, Peterson, and Roelfs (1974) study sponsored by the Commission on Non-Traditional Study reported a participation rate of 31 percent. However, by adjusting this figure upward to include the higher rate of participation (an estimated 3 percent per year between 1972 and 1979) as well as the College Board respondent bias toward higher income, more education, and advanced occupations; and adjusting it downward to account for an age range of 18 to 60 years rather than the age range of 25 years and older used by the College Board, the figures probably would converge.

Similar adjustments made in other studies conducted by Johnstone and Rivera (1965), Moses (1970), Tough (1971), and Penland (1977) would produce comparable results. In short, depending on the age group studied and the definition of learning applied, a reasonable current estimate of the rate of adult participation in learning is about 50 percent.

Profile of Learners and Nonlearners

An examination of the characteristics of learners and nonlearners among the survey participants showed a number of differences — differences that confirmed once again what earlier studies have repeatedly found. The contrasts between the two groups are discussed here:

- *Learners are considerably younger than nonlearners.* Twice as many learners as nonlearners come from the group 25 to 29 years of age, while only half as many come from the group aged 65 to 69. Half of all adult learners are under 40 (Table 2).[1]

- *Learners are considerably better educated than nonlearners.* Adults who have gone beyond high school are twice as likely to learn as those who have not. Only about one out of five with eight years of school or less participate in learning (Table 3).

- *Adults with high incomes are more likely to learn.* Twice as many learners as nonlearners are from families earning $25,000 a year or more. The breakpoint comes at family incomes of $10,000 or more: above it, learners outnumber nonlearners; below it, nonlearners outnumber learners.

---

1. The tables cited in this and the following chapters appear in Appendix A.

There is no income ceiling on learning; 2 out of 3 adults from families earning $50,000 a year or more are engaged in learning (Table 4).

- *Employed adults are far more likely to engage in learning than unemployed adults.* Those who are working full-time are even more likely to learn than those who work part-time. Less than 1 out of 3 retirees is engaged in learning. In short, the more work a person is doing, the more likely he or she is to engage in learning (Table 5).

- *Of all occupational groups, adults engaged in professional and technical work are most likely to learn, while those in farm work are least likely.* There is a clear relationship between the amount of training required to enter an occupation and the need or desire to continue learning (Table 6).

- *Adults employed in business and professional fields are more likely to engage in learning than those employed in agriculture, mining, construction, and transportation* (Table 7).

- *Single adults who have never married and divorced adults are more likely to engage in learning than others, while widowed adults are less likely to participate* (Table 8).

- *Women with children under the age of 18 are considerably more likely to engage in learning than women with children over 18* (Table 9).

- *Participation in learning drops sharply among adults who have five or more children.* The learning of adults with fewer than five children is unaffected by the number (Table 10).

- *Blacks supply considerably less than their proportionate share of learners; Hispanics supply their share; whites supply more than their share; other groups — Orientals, American Indians, etc. — supply considerably more than their share* (Table 11).

- *Learners are slightly more likely to live in urbanized areas.* Adult participation in learning is below average in places with a population of less than 2,500 and in rural areas (Table 12).

- *Adults in the Pacific Coast states are more likely to engage in learning than those in any other region of the nation, while adults in the South Atlantic states are less likely to participate than in any other region* (Table 13).

• *There are no differences in adult learning according to sex or number of persons in the household 25 years of age or older* (Tables 14 and 15).

While there are demographic differences between learners and nonlearners, some large and some small, they do not appear to be decisive determinants of whether adults will learn. There are, after all, many adult learners who are older, are black, are poorly educated, have low incomes or low-level occupations, or who live in rural areas not on the Pacific Coast. They must have something in common with other learners that has the power to explain why all of them learn.

In short, demographic characteristics can help describe adult learners but they cannot explain *why* adults learn. The demographic characteristics of learners are correlated with the causes, but are not themselves the causes, of adult learning.

5

REASONS FOR ADULT LEARNING

Why are half of all adults engaged in learning? We asked the learners surveyed to give us their reasons.

Life Changes as Reasons for Learning

An impressive 83 percent of the learners surveyed described some past, present, or future change in their lives as reasons to learn. They talked about learning to use new machines their companies had acquired, learning the histories of the churches they were joining, learning to take care of their aging parents in declining health, learning tennis now that they had moved to the suburbs, or learning how to give up smoking when so ordered by their doctors. In short, they talked about how their lives had changed, were changing, or would change and how they had to learn to cope with those changes.

Other Reasons for Learning

The remaining 17 percent surveyed did not cite changes in their lives as causing them to learn. Instead, they said they were learning for other reasons: for example, because they found learning to be a satisfying activity, because it kept them mentally alert, because it gave them a chance to be with other adults, because it gave them something to do with their children, because their friends had asked them to join in learning, because they admired the teacher, or simply because it filled up their time.

Many of the 17 percent made it clear that the experience of acquiring the knowledge was as important to them as the satisfaction of possessing it. The social aspects of learning—the chance to get out of the house, meet people, talk with other learners—were important to some. The stimulation of learning—the mental and physical challenge, hearing the thinking of the teachers, watching the performance of other students—was important to some. The sense of engaging actively in something—in contrast to spending more passive evenings in front of the television set—was important to some. For those people, the quality of the learning experience mattered as much as or more than the aftereffect.

A number of the 17 percent who did not attribute their learning to any change in their lives described themselves as continuous learners, pointing out that they had always learned as a normal part of living. Some said they were continuing studies they had begun years earlier, perhaps in childhood. Bible study was mentioned more often than anything else as a topic of continuous study. Other learners moved immediately from one topic to another without a break. One woman named gourmet cooking, home decorating, needlepoint, and furniture refinishing courses as her most recent four in a long series of courses.

Some of the 17 percent seemed to engage in learning because it was a part of their self-image. They described themselves as constant (if not "lifelong") learners. The following comment was typical:

> I'm always learning something—always have, always will. I'm not a person who can just sit around. I really think a person has to learn to stay alive.

A few of the 17 percent said that they learned or developed new skills simply because it made them feel competent to have those skills. For those people, the learning activity itself was not as important as the result of the study. They were a bit like collectors for whom the collection is more important than the acts of collecting. These people were a minority.

Contrasts in the Reasons

In short, 83 percent of the adults interviewed said that they were learning in order to cope with a life change, while 17 percent said they were learning for other reasons (see Figure 7).

Figure 7: REASONS FOR LEARNING

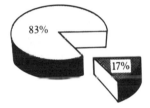

☐ Learning to cope with life changes
▓ Other reasons

(Also appears as Table 16 in Appendix A.)

That important distinction can be expressed in several different ways:

- *17 percent learned for the sake of the learning experience; 83 percent learned for the sake of something else.*

- *17 percent regarded the learning activity itself as the benefit they wanted; 83 percent were learning to obtain some other benefit.*

- *17 percent got their satisfaction during the learning experience, apart from any later effect; 83 percent got their satisfaction from a later effect.*

- *83 percent wanted some reward from learning; 17 percent regarded the process of learning or the possession of knowledge to be its own reward.*

- *For 83 percent, learning was utilitarian; for 17 percent, learning was its own justification.*

- *For 83 percent, learning was the means; for 17 percent, learning was the end.*

Transitions as Reasons for Learning

The bulk of the data supported our hypothesis that most adults learn in order to move out of some status they must or wish to leave and into some new status they must or wish to enter. That is, their reason for learning was to perform well in the new status.

As we heard them tell their stories about learning, we knew what other investigators would have said if they had been listening. Sheehy would have used the term *passages* to describe their shifts from one status to another. Vaillant would have observed that they were moving through stages. Neugarten would have heard the twin ticking of the biological and the social clocks. Schlossberg would have heard vivid examples of crisis and adaptation and coping and stress during the transitions, many requiring adults to learn as a way of responding; she would have seen again how the characteristics of the individual and the circumstances and the transition determined whether the adult would learn enough to succeed in the new status. Lowenthal, Thurnher, and Chiriboga would have said again:

> The anticipation of an impending transition often serves as a stimulus to examine, and possibly to reorient, goals and aspirations, and to reassess personal resources and impediments in the light of the probability of their attainment. (1975, p. x)

But they might have added something similar to: *The result of this reassessment for many adults is the realization that they will have to learn something new if they are going to make the transition successfully.* Listening to the interviews, Gould would have noted again that adult life is not a plateau and that the road traversing it is not level and straight. He might have added that adults have to learn new ways of traveling when the road changes sharply. Hearing the interviews, Levinson would have reminded us that life is not a single season and that adults have to live differently in each season. He might have said "live and learn" in each season or, more perceptively, "learn to live" in each season.

Transitions: Past, Present, and Future

Some transitions thrust adults suddenly into new circumstances before they have learned how to succeed in their new situations. Their learning follows their transitions. Other transitions occur more slowly, allowing adults time to accommodate to their changing circumstances by learning as their circumstances change. Their learning accompanies their transitions. Some transitions can be anticipated, at times years in advance, and some adults choose to learn in anticipation of making a change. Their learning precedes their transitions. The adults we talked with gave examples of all three types of transitions—past, present, and future—as causing them to learn.

Divorce came on a variable schedule, sometimes expected, sometimes surprising. The same was true for job changes, deaths in the family, changes in personal health, the birth of children, and many others. In contrast were the transitions that could always be anticipated and prepared for (not that every adult prepared). Those included marriage, the entry of a child into kindergarten or college, and the retirement of the adult or a spouse.

Kinds of Transitions Requiring Learning

We took the reasons given by those who said they were learning to make some past, present, or future life transition and classified them into the seven life areas in which we had hypothesized that transitions would occur: career, family, health, religion, citizenship, art, and leisure. The results of that analysis showed that while adults are learning to make transitions in every life area, more are learning because of transitions in some areas than in others. Thus, learning is unevenly distributed over the categories (see Figure 8).

CAREER. A large majority of the reasons given by those who said they were in transition turned out to be related to their careers: 56 percent named career transitions as their reasons

Figure 8: **TRANSITIONS REQUIRING LEARNING**

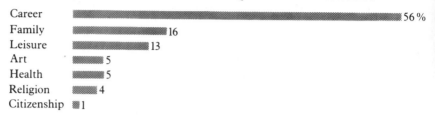

Career 56%
Family 16
Leisure 13
Art 5
Health 5
Religion 4
Citizenship .1

Percentages above represent the 83 percent who gave life changes as their reasons for learning. For example, 56 percent of the 83 percent who cited life changes named transitions in their careers.

(Also appears as Table 17 in Appendix A.)

for deciding to learn. Career transitions, thus, outnumbered all others combined as reasons for learning.

FAMILY. Transitions in their family lives were mentioned by 16 percent of those who said they were learning. While family transitions ranked second to career transitions as reasons for learning, they were a distant second.

LEISURE. Almost as many — 13 percent — pointed to transitions in their leisure patterns as forcing them to decide to learn something new. Again, although leisure ranked third as a reason for learning, only one person learned because of a leisure transition for every four persons who learned because of career transitions.

ART. Few people gave transitions in their esthetic lives as making them decide to learn. Only 5 percent of all the reasons given by those in transition could be classified as esthetic.

HEALTH. Few people reported transitions in their general health as necessitating learning. Only 5 percent gave reasons falling into this category.

RELIGION. Still fewer people — about 4 percent — said that their religious lives had shifted enough to require new learning. (We found that many of those engaged in religious study did so as the habit of a lifetime rather than because of some recent past, present, or anticipated future transition in their religious lives.)

CITIZENSHIP. Almost none of the reasons — fewer than 1 percent — had anything to do with a transition in citizenship status, such as a shift in a political party, a sudden increase in level of political activity, or the application for United States citizenship by the foreign born.

Summary

More adults learn in order to make career transitions than for all other reasons combined, with family and leisure transitions competing for a distant second place. No other life area accounted for more than 5 percent of the transitions requiring learning.

Triggers as Times for Learning

What about the timing of learning — the reason for learning now rather than at some earlier or later point in time? Had anything happened in the lives of the 60 million adult learners sampled in our survey to cause them to learn in the previous 12 months rather than sooner or later? What about the notion of specific life events triggering learning, the notion that we expanded into a clear hypothesis?

The adults surveyed who said they were learning something currently or had learned something in the last 12 months were asked in the following questions to explain their timing:

- When did you start learning?
- Why did you start then?
- Why not earlier?
- Why not later?
- What happened at that time to cause you to start then?

As we had hypothesized, all the adults who named transitions in their lives as motivating them to learn could also point to specific events triggering their decisions to learn currently rather than sooner or later. Levinson's concept of "marker events" as milestones dividing the life course into segments gains solid support from our survey results, as does Lowenthal's concept of "stressors." Transitions are marked by identifiable events, and it is the timing of these events that causes many adults to decide to learn now rather than at some other point in time. The finding that life events trigger decisions to learn now is fully consistent with the finding that life transitions establish reasons to learn. The logical chain is as follows: (1) transitions require learning; (2) identifiable events mark the occurrence of those transitions; and (3) those events determine the times for learning.

The triggering events cited by the adults surveyed were sometimes cataclysmic, such as a contested divorce, getting fired, or the death of a loved one. But sometimes they were lesser, yet still significant events, such as the last child leaving for college, getting promoted to the next rung on a career ladder, or moving to a new town. In any case, the adults with whom we talked who attributed their learning to transitions in their lives had little trouble in singling out the events that made them decide to learn when they did.

Kinds of Events Triggering Learning

We took the life events mentioned by the adults interviewed as making them decide to learn at a particular point in time and classified them into the seven life areas listed earlier: career, family, health, religion, citizenship, art, and leisure. In one respect, the results looked much like those we found when we classified life transitions into the same seven life areas: once again, 56 percent of the triggering events related to careers. But in other respects, the results were different: family life doubled in size as an arena for triggering events; artistic life disappeared; and leisure life evaporated. There was little change in the health, religion, or citizenship areas. While they had accounted for few life transitions requiring learning, they accounted for even fewer triggering events causing learning at a particular point in time (see Figure 9). After a careful ex-

Figure 9: TRIGGERS FOR LEARNING

Career	▨▨▨▨▨▨▨▨▨▨▨▨▨▨▨▨▨▨▨▨▨ 56%
Family	▨▨▨▨▨▨▨▨▨▨▨▨ 36
Health	▨ 4
Religion	▨ 2
Citizenship	▨ 1

Percentages above represent the 83 percent who gave life changes as their reasons for learning. For example, 36 percent of the 83 percent who cited life changes named triggering events in their family life. Triggers in Art and Leisure were given by less than one-half of one percent of the respondents.

(Also appears as Table 18 in Appendix A.)

amination of the data, we believe that the interpretation of these findings is quite straightforward.

CAREER. Career transitions are usually marked by career-related events. Moving up a career ladder is marked by a series of promotions coming at identifiable points in time. Changing jobs is marked by the termination of one and the beginning of another, two career events that can usually be timed to the hour. The need to learn more about a job is usually associated with a specific career event such as the arrival of new equipment, the new opening of an office or plant, the addition of new personnel to be supervised, or the enactment of a new law requiring credit to get a license renewed. The result is that career transitions requiring learning tend to be accompanied by career events requiring learning at a particular time. Thus, it is not surprising that 56 percent of all transitions requiring learning are in the career area and that (with an exactness that we attribute to coincidence) 56 percent of the events triggering learning are in the career area.

There are exceptions, of course. Not every transition requiring learning about a career is accompanied by a triggering event in the career area. Consider the young man who marries, has to change jobs to support his family, and has to learn to make a successful transition to the new job. His family event has triggered his career transition. Or consider the young woman who is forced to go to work when her father dies and leaves no money to pay her college tuition. Her family event has triggered her career transition. Despite such exceptions as these, however, there is a close correspondence between career transitions and career triggers.

FAMILY. There are twice as many family events triggering learning as there are family transitions requiring learning. This is because many changes in an adult's relations with family members require learning something outside family life, while few changes outside family life require learning new family skills. Examples of the first include the divorced woman who must learn a career in order to earn an independent income, the new widower who wants to learn dancing so he can find new friends, and the troubled parents whose son is killed in wartime and who turn to religious learning for solace. Thus, family living is rich in triggering events leading to transitions in other life areas, which in turn require learning in those life areas.

HEALTH. We found a virtual one-to-one correspondence between a transition in a person's health and a triggering event occurring in that person's health area. Those events ordinarily consisted of traumatic health changes such as heart attacks or accidental injuries such as broken legs. For this reason, health transitions and health triggers each accounted for about 5 percent of adult learning.

RELIGION. Few religious transitions (only 4 percent) were cited by those interviewed as reasons for learning and even fewer identifiable events in their religious lives (only 2 percent) were cited as reasons for learning at a particular point in time. This means that life events in other areas such as family or health triggered half of all religious transitions. What usually happened in such cases was that the adult had undergone a highly significant life-changing event, which caused a reexamination of his or her relationship with God. Such events included major defeats in secular life such as loss of job, spouse, child, and major secular events that brought death closer such as serious illness or serious injury. However, they also included lesser events such as deciding to marry a person of another faith and attending religious classes in that person's church or synagogue to learn a new faith.

CITIZENSHIP. Just as only 1 percent of the adults interviewed named citizenship transitions as causing them to learn, only 1 percent named triggering events in the citizenship area as causing them to learn at a particular point in time. Those events included a foreign person's decision to apply for United States citizenship and a citizen's volunteering to serve in a neighborhood action group.

LEISURE AND ART ACTIVITIES. While 18 percent of the adults interviewed attributed their learning to transitions in their leisure (13 percent) or artistic lives (5 percent), less than one-half of 1 percent pointed to any event in their leisure activities or artistic pursuits that triggered their decisions to learn at a particular point in time.

As we explain earlier, our interpretation of this finding is that adult Americans think of leisure as leftover time, time when everything that must be done has been done and that can be used for leisure activities. This means that the amount of leisure time adults have is a direct function of their life obligations. That is, leisure expands as other life obligations contract, and leisure contracts as other life obligations expand. It is the events in the arena of those obligations that the adult associates with changes in leisure time or leisure activities. Thus when an adult finds himself or herself with more or less leisure time or undertakes new leisure activities, the adult identifies an event in his or her primary life space (rather than his or her leisure space) as triggering the leisure transition and the learning needed to accomplish it.

We believe that most adults regard artistic activities in the same way as leisure activities: options to be pursued if, but only if, all obligations have been met. The pattern we see in leisure activities seems to apply to artistic activities: It is events in the arena of life obligations that expand or contract the time available for engaging in music, dance, painting, or theater. Thus, when an adult undertakes new learning in the arts, he or she identifies an event in a life area other than the arts as triggering the artistic learning.

In short, adults associate leisure learning or artistic learning with triggering events taking place in other life areas. This explains the distinct difference between the 18 percent who attribute their learning to transitions in their leisure or artistic lives and the less than 1 percent who identify triggering events in those same life areas.

SUMMARY. More than 90 percent of the events triggering adult learning occur in career or family life. Evidently the career clock and the family clock set the time for learning.

Solid Support for the Notion of Latent Learning

We had hypothesized that a considerable amount of adult learning is latent: adults have undergone, are undergoing, or want to undergo transitions that require them to learn, but learning has not come because the circumstances are not right. The survey results confirmed the hypothesis that the decision to learn at a certain point in time is triggered by specific events. It was quite common for adults to explain their decisions to learn at a particular time by beginning their explanations with such statements as:

> Well, I had been thinking for a long time about taking more accounting courses and going back to work, but I couldn't because the kids were too little. Then when my youngest got out of elementary school and started junior high, I felt all the kids were pretty well set and would be spending less time at home and needing less attention from me. That's when I knew the time had come to complete my accounting degree.

In short, the findings confirmed what we suspected: need, opportunity, and even desire are not sufficient to cause most adults to learn at a particular point in time. Something must happen to convert most latent adult learners into active learners. If the events had occurred earlier or later, the learning would have been triggered earlier or later. Thus, we are led to conclude that there are millions of potential adult learners and that the timing of their entry into the learning arena is determined by specific events in their lives which permit them — or force them — to enter it. To know an adult's life schedule is to know an adult's learning schedule.

The Connection Between Transitions and Triggers

We had hypothesized that while the topic an adult chooses to learn is always related to the transition requiring that learning, the topic is not always related to the event triggering that learning. The findings of the survey supported that hypothesis as well. One adult interviewed had suffered a heart attack, a cataclysmic, life-changing, triggering event, which forced him to enter a less strenuous occupation. This major transition required him to learn something new. While the triggering event had to do with his health, the topic he chose to learn had to do with the career transition he was forced to make.

Another adult interviewed had just experienced a significant event in her family life, an event triggering a major transition: her aged mother had become seriously ill and had moved into her home. The mother needed nursing care that the daughter could not afford; nursing care the daughter could supply if she were trained. The triggering event for the daughter's learning took place in her family life; the topic of her daughter's learning had to do with health care. As it was for many adults, the event triggering the learning took place in one area of life while the topic of learning involved another area of life.

We feel that the distinction is important for those who provide adult learning. They should not expect that divorce will automatically lead an adult to study family relations: the adult may learn secretarial skills instead. They should not expect that a job promotion will lead an adult to study the occupation: the adult instead may learn to sail the new boat he purchased with the salary raise. They should not expect retirement to lead an adult to study leisure activities: the adult instead may learn a new relationship with God in anticipation of the final life transition.

Life Schedules as Determinants
of Reasons and Times for Learning

When we first saw the statistics on transitions and triggers, we immediately thought that we could explain why they were not divided equally in all life areas. We assumed that adults find their careers and family lives more turbulent than the other aspects of their lives and thus as producing more changes requiring learning. But we were wrong. The explanation is even simpler which we discovered while analyzing adults' answers to a question about how much time they spend in each of the seven life areas. Table 19 shows that adults trace about 80 percent of their learning (70 percent of their transitions and 90 percent of their triggering events for an average of 80 percent) to changes in career and family life and that they spend about 80 percent of their time with their careers and families. This close correspondence suggests a cause and effect relationship between how adults spend their lives and the changes in their lives that cause them to learn.

Several other interesting facts are shown in Table 19. One is that careers are evidently somewhat more turbulent than family life, judging from the fact that careers cause more learning in proportion to time spent in them. The same is true for personal health: Americans spend only about 2 percent of their time taking care of their health, but credit health changes with causing 5 percent of their learning. Perhaps if more time were spent taking care of health, adults would have fewer health changes requiring new knowledge, skills, or attitudes.

Another noteworthy item in Table 19 is that adults spend 16 percent of their waking hours at leisure, yet they rarely name leisure events as triggering new learning. Our interpretation of this fact is that leisure is, by definition, the absence of required activity. Adults seem to regard it as just that, leftover time. When their leisure expands or contracts, as it often does, adults attribute it to changes in other life areas, such as work or family. Similarly, when they name a new leisure activity they have learned, they trace the learning to an event in the other life area that changed their leisure time and their leisure activities. For example, an adult who has a heart attack and is forced to learn golf as a substitute for tennis traces the new learning to an event in personal health rather than to an event in leisure pursuits. In short, Americans do not regard expansions or contractions in their leisure time as something accomplished by taking direct action on leisure, but rather as something accomplished by taking direct action in other areas of their lives, such as by reducing their work time or increasing their church or community activities. They see their leisure learning triggered by nonleisure events.

Another finding in Table 19 merits a note of explanation: adults spend almost no time in artistic activities yet spend 5 percent of their time learning about art. How is this? The explanation is that while we classified certain activities as artistic, the adults interviewed classified them as leisure (for example, ballet lessons, art history courses, piano lessons, etc.). Adults use these artistic pursuits for leisure purposes.

A look at adult learning in the various life areas provides myriad illustrations of the predominant learning patterns.

EXAMPLES OF TRANSITIONS AND TRIGGERING EVENTS

The adult learners interviewed described hundreds of transitions and triggering events scattered across every area of their lives. In this chapter we look at some samples of what they said. Each sample of adult learning consists of a transition and a trigger embedded in a segment of conversation telling what and how (and often when, where, from whom, and with whom) the adult was learning. Although the what and how are usually the most vivid and detailed information in the case, only the transition and the triggering event are the subject of the accompanying discussion. For that reason, the cases are organized into seven life areas according to the nature of the *transition* rather than the nature of the *trigger* or the *topic* of learning. The examples are further categorized within each life area to show the various kinds of transitions we found.

Changes in Careers

Adult learners gave dozens of examples of how going through transitions in their careers required them to learn something new. Many of those transitions were voluntary; some were not. It followed that while many adults wanted to learn, others had to learn.

Most career transitions fell into these three categories: (1) moving into a new job, (2) adapting to a changing job, and (3) advancing in a career. The natural chronology of career entry and career progression is quite evident here: Many adults had to learn in order to get their jobs, keep them, or advance beyond them.

Most of the specific events triggering the decisions to make career transitions at particular points in time occurred at work.

Most fell into five categories: (1) getting hired; (2) having an existing job change, as through the arrival of new equipment or the passage of new regulations; (3) being offered advancement; (4) getting promoted; and (5) stopping work. On the other hand, some of the events triggering career transitions took place in other life areas. For example, the decision to seek a promotion sometimes sprang from an event unrelated to work, such as having a baby and needing more income.

Some examples of transitions and triggers, organized according to transition categories, follow.

MOVING INTO A NEW JOB. Many adults explained that taking a new job—or beginning an entirely new career—required them to learn after they started to work in order to become fully qualified. For example,

> I had been out of work for six months, and then I had the chance to get a job as a medical research assistant in the hospital. I had had a lot of experience in my past jobs as a medical technologist doing all sorts of analyses on blood samples. But, this hospital was small, so I was not only responsible for running tests on the patient's blood samples, but also drawing the blood myself. I had to take a course in phlebotomy at the medical center before I could do my job completely.

> . . .

> First, I was a criminologist. I worked in the prison as a correctional officer and I evaluated prisoners' progress. That job was too hard for me; it was a terrible job and dangerous as well. People were getting killed in the prison and there were riots. I couldn't stay in that occupation, so I gave it up and looked for a very low stress area. Now, I'm working on my Master's degree in library science and working in a small library in Florida.

Anyone who is 20 years old today can expect to make six or seven job changes over the course of his or her working life. Based on this frequency and the rate of predicted change in the nature and requirements of jobs in years to follow, many adults will join this medical research assistant and prospective librarian in seeking further training to handle new tasks or entirely new jobs.

Other adults said they had to learn new skills before they could even seek new jobs. Often, family events triggered the decision to learn new job skills. Three examples follow.

This woman's youngest child had just begun kindergarten, prompting her decision to go back to work.

> I'm unemployed now and I'm going back to teaching art. I want to give private lessons again. Last spring I took a class, a two-day seminar, on starting a new business at the university extension. I took it because I was starting to set up my own studio and wanted to know all about taxes and other things about running a business of my own separate from my husband's business.

She is not the only woman reentering the labor force who is finding it necessary to learn. By 1990, 60 percent of all adult women will be at work, compared with the 50 percent or so who now work. Like this woman, many of the other new entrants will find that the road to work runs through the schoolhouse.

Many adults told us that they had been influenced by advice or suggestions from good friends or family members and had decided to learn for that reason. Frequently, those conversations with friends or family crystalized long-held ideas or wishes.

> I finished a course in real estate, took the state exam, and got my license to practice. A friend triggered it all. She is a broker and I hadn't seen her in a while. We played golf and were having lunch. She kept saying, "Dottie, you ought to sell houses." Actually, I have several friends in the real estate business who told me I should go into real estate because I like people and I like houses. I talked about it with another friend and she said, "Let's do it together." So, we looked at different schools and the cost and enrolled in one five minutes from my house and now I'm a broker.

The large number of women entering or reentering the labor force may be producing a chain reaction, influencing their friends to do likewise. Many adults told us that going to school together was companionable and reassuring after years outside the classroom. We also found that adults receive advice from their parents. Some adults 25 to 35 years of age started learning because their parents suggested it. Others started at the initiative of their husbands or wives and sometimes their children. Family approval and support seemed important to many adults.

A trigger sometimes came in the form of the removal of active family opposition to learning. An adult who moves out of an atmosphere of nonsupport may suddenly be free to learn.

> I got a divorce at about the time my youngest child, Abby, turned 5. I had wanted to go back to school before that, but my husband didn't want me to. He was content that I stay at home. I didn't want to—so that was a bone of contention between us. Then, when I got my divorce, I was able to get away from diapers and dishes. Back to school I went and with my ambition and some luck, I'll be a paralegal in six months.

One of the most dramatic events an adult can experience is divorce. Many adults pointed to recent divorces as causing them to learn when they did. In this case, divorce allowed the woman to continue an education that marriage had interrupted. Often divorce provides the obligation. Other adults told of being forced into the labor market when divorce deprived them of their incomes or raised their expenses in the form of alimony payments. Whether divorce permits or requires learning, the rising rate of divorce and separation among married couples can be expected to lead to more adult learning.

ADAPTING TO A CHANGING JOB. Many adults explained that their existing jobs had changed—sometimes suddenly—and that such changes had triggered the need to learn simply in order to keep their jobs.

> I work in the post office operating a machine that keys all the mail that comes through. They're always changing things so we're being trained again. They make changes all the time to handle more mail coming through. I have to get trained on the

new machine they've brought in. If I didn't want to be trained, I would have to quit the job and take a lower-paying job sorting mail by hand.

.   .   .

I teach deaf children using sign language. The children I usually teach are around 6 to 8 years old and my level of sign language is fine for them. But, funding for the school was cut back and the different grade levels for deaf children had to be combined. Now I am responsible for teaching children ranging from 6 to 15 years old. I needed to be able to converse at higher levels and more fluently. That's why I enrolled in the course in sign language. Next year, I might even be teaching in the high school, who knows. But at least I'll be prepared for the next job change.

.   .   .

I work as a secretary at an insurance company. They needed a better way of handling claims. So many claims come in and they need to verify the accident details, injuries, and medical bills — things like that. So, they installed computers to handle the load. Now instead of filing the information I had to put it into the computer. That involved keypunching. I knew nothing about keypunching, so they paid my way to go to classes that were offered by the company who furnished the computers.

.   .   .

I graduated with a degree in teaching, decided against teaching, and got a job in business. When I was going through four years of college, learning how to teach students American history, I missed a lot of math courses and other subjects I now use daily on the job. I'm taking a U.S. Department of Commerce course in advanced export administration. I'm in the export business and my job has grown by leaps and bounds — more commodities and more countries to deal with. I need to improve my administrative skills so I can keep up with the expansion in my job.

Running faster to stay in the same place requires continual learning, especially in occupational fields with changing technologies, changing government regulations, changing markets, or intense competition. That is why adults with professional, managerial, and technical jobs are twice as likely to learn as those in, for example, mining and construction.

ADVANCING IN A CAREER. Many adults who were interested in career advancement discovered that they had to learn in order to advance. For some, getting a promotion and assuming new responsibilities often triggered the need to learn a new skill. For others, the triggers came in different forms: they included seeing peers move ahead, having a boss suggest that they get ready for a future promotion, and a change in family circumstances requiring higher incomes.

Promotions do not always reflect a worker's qualifications. Employers often advance personnel for reasons other than the fact that they are prepared for their new assignments; such reasons include seniority, labor shortages, and desirable work traits and attitudes. Training then becomes necessary. Sometimes the employer provides the training; sometimes the employee arranges for the training outside the place of employment; and sometimes both do their share.

A promotion for this secretary was followed by the need to learn shorthand in order to succeed.

> I started out as a receptionist. Then, I got promoted to executive secretary. My first position did not require that I do shorthand, but when I got promoted, I found myself in a situation that meant I had to take dictation. Being a small organization, my boss was a very considerate person and kept telling me, "Look, try taking the dictation. We'll work on this together." Well, I continued in this way, very nervously, and decided it was time to take a course in shorthand. What an improvement!

The primary purpose of employer-supplied adult training is to equip workers to do what they have already been hired to do. But not all adults take jobs before they are ready to do them. Some adults learn now in order to lay a foundation for eventual promotion. The learning tends to come in the early years in a new job when an adult anticipates that new skills will help in the future. Thus it is a stronger motive among younger people who see promotion as a possibility, where there is a clear occupational hierarchy offering visible chances for advancement, or where pay is directly connected to performance, as in certain sales jobs.

The decision to learn ahead of time can be triggered by specific events at work such as seeing better-trained workers get better job offers and bigger raises.

> I'm taking a financial management course to apply toward my MBA. I want an MBA to make me more marketable. I'm in personnel so I see how marketable an MBA makes people. I'm very satisfied with my job, but I haven't gotten a decent raise in three years. Changing jobs is almost a sure fire way to get a raise and the way things are with the cost of living, I may need to change. The MBA will give me an edge if I shift jobs. Of course, it will also give me a better job and a raise if I stay where I am.

Degrees can increase an adult's competitive edge in a difficult job market, as many people find, whether they want to advance in their present place of employment or go elsewhere. Especially for people who are young, energetic, and ambitious, learning looks like the route to advancement. That is one reason learning is more common among those under 35 years of age than among those over 55.

Another event that is highly likely to trigger an adult's decision to learn in advance is a current employer's request—or requirement—that the adult get additional training, especially if a clear change in status will follow that learning.

> I'm an electrician and I took a course in electrical estimating put on by the Electrical Contractors' Association. My boss asked me to take the course because he plans to bring me into the office and make me an estimator. Since I took the course, he's had me spend some time in the office doing the beginning phases of electrical estimating.

A request or even a requirement from an employer is, of course, not mandatory. The worker can always quit rather than comply. When workers do comply with their employers' requests or requirements, it is usually to retain their jobs or to advance their careers.

Changes in Family Life

Adult learners gave other examples of how changes in their families caused them to begin learning. Most changes could be readily classified into the following categories of family living: (1) providing different food; (2) providing different shelter; (3) providing different clothing; (4) managing shifts in family income and expenses; and (5) caring for other family members when changes occur. That is, if we use an admittedly simplistic view of traditional family life — the life being lived by most of the adults we interviewed — we can envision a house or an apartment with two or more family members who care for each other gaining and spending income to provide food, shelter, and clothing. From time to time there are changes, some voluntary and some involuntary, which stimulate or require them to learn more so that they can cope with or take advantage of new circumstances.

Major events in the family lives of adults often trigger their decisions to make family transitions at certain times. Most of the events fall into the following 12 categories:

1. Getting married
2. Becoming pregnant
3. Children moving through school
4. Getting divorced
5. Moving to a new location
6. Acquiring a new house or apartment
7. Increase in family income
8. Direction from friends or family
9. Rising cost of living
10. Injury or illness of a family member
11. Retirement of a spouse
12. Death of a family member

The natural chronology of major family life events — getting married, becoming pregnant, having children, moving to a new location, acquiring a new house, having children go through school, having the husband or wife retire, and death of a family member — is apparent in the family life triggers mentioned by more than one-third of all adults interviewed as causing them to learn. Some family triggering events required learning; others permitted adults to begin learning things they had wanted to learn for a long time. In either case, they saw learning as a way to succeed in the new status they were entering.

Few events triggering family transitions come from other life areas. The primary exception is retirement. Frequently, stopping work was found to be associated with an adult's decision to learn family-related topics.

Some examples of transitions and triggers, organized according to transition categories, follow.

PROVIDING FOOD. Learning how to prepare food—or learning how to prepare it differently—can be triggered by any number of events. One is a drop in family income or a rise in family expenses. Because eating habits allow for considerable discretion, adjusting them is a relatively easy and instantaneous way of dealing with a sudden change in family finances.

> I first got interested in baking and canning when all the prices began going up. My husband had had a couple of heart attacks and a lot of medical bills rolled in. Six months he was out of work last year. So I decided to make my own bread. In fact, my daughter really started me doing it because she baked some bread and I got it in my head that she was not going to be able to do it over me. So I started doing it. It is satisfying and it saves money.

If rising costs trigger learning, we can be confident that adult learning will continue to increase.

Another event which triggers the decision to provide food differently is moving to a new location.

> I had helped my parents raise vegetables when I was a little boy, so I had not forgotten how good fresh vegetables taste. But, until I started raising a family of my own and became concerned about the additives in the food my children were eating and the prices I was paying for food, I did not stop to consider how much better and cheaper it would be to raise our own food. When we moved into the country and had a little bit of land, I decided now was the time to do it. But, I hadn't retained enough knowledge of raising food from my younger days, so I needed some help. They were offering agriculture extension courses and I enrolled.

The current wave of adult interest in better nutrition will lead other adults to learn more in order to eat better.

PROVIDING SHELTER. Many adults explained that buying a house or moving into a new apartment—particularly the former—had started their learning.

> I moved into a house that had been there since 1953 and nobody had touched it since. It had the original countertops and I couldn't even get the sink clean. There was a huge stove that took up all the space and left nowhere to work. But the house needed a new roof and I had to pay for that first. I had already

> priced the cost of getting the kitchen redone and it was too expensive. Then one day I walked into the kitchen to cook a cake and the stove did not work. That was it. I went out and got a part-time job. Even then, I knew I would have to do most of the work myself. I'm learning mostly with how-to-do-it books from the library. I decide what I need to do and then get it. Then I bother everybody I know who has ever done anything similar. I've put in a sink, stove, countertops, windows, all the plumbing.

Fixing up an old house can be fun or even necessary. The do-it-yourself era is getting a new boost from the rising costs of repair and construction. It may get another boost from the rapidly growing number of retired people on fixed incomes. Doing it yourself often means learning it yourself.

Some adults said that a salary raise, or perhaps the wife entering the labor market and bringing in a second income, enabled them to start a new activity requiring learning.

> I got a good raise at the plant. That let me go out and buy a new set of power tools for my wood shop. That meant that I could begin making furniture for myself—new things as well as fixing old things—refinishing, repairing, and so on. So, I'm taking furniture-making lessons at the high school now so that I can get the benefits of my new tools.

Sometimes, as in this case, higher incomes let adults begin something that they have wanted to do for a long time. In other cases, higher incomes precipitate an unplanned change in life style that requires new learning, often in how to use leisure more expensively.

The energy crisis has and will continue to motivate adults to adjust to shortages. Learning about alternative energy sources and changing current practices will be attractive to many adults.

> With all the talk of the energy problem and the oil crisis and the heating bills, I had decided I had had enough. I read an article in a magazine about solar heating and then I found out that our electrical and gas company would give us a rebate for implementing a solar heating system in our house, plus the cost could be deducted from our income tax, I said why not. Our house was in a perfect location for solar energy and our kids had left home, so we only had to heat the downstairs. But, I needed the know-how and technical information. The field is so new and I needed

expert advice on what to buy and how to put it in. That's what these manuals on solar heating are giving me.

Not everybody will go in for do-it-yourself solar heating, of course. But many adults are going to have to learn how to keep their shelters warm in the future without spending an excessive portion of their incomes doing it.

PROVIDING CLOTHING. Like eating, dressing allows substantial room for discretion. It is easy to buy more or less and to pay more or less as income and other expenses rise or fall. Most of the adults we interviewed talked about accommodating their wardrobes to rising expenses.

It's called fabric and finance — over at the high school adult ed. We study best buys in clothes and go on shopping trips every fourth week to places where you can get really good quality at a price. My money for clothes doesn't go as far as it did. I have to stretch every dollar and "cheap but quality" is the way to do it.

We found other adults learning how to make clothing rather than buy it as yet another way of beating prices. The arrival of children in a family sometimes prompts women to learn to sew.

When I gave birth to our second child when I was 40, my husband and I were so excited. But all our children were grown, and there were no "hand-me-downs" for this one. Well, unlike raising the older three, there were no other children in the house so I had a little more time, plus the fact I did not want to pay the prices for children's clothes these days—clothes they would outgrow fast enough. So, when the baby was old enough to leave with my oldest daughter, I enrolled in a basic sewing course at our local YWCA.

Whether for themselves or for their children, whether by buying or by sewing, some adults will continue seeking better ways of stretching their clothing budgets.

MANAGING SHIFTS IN FAMILY INCOME AND EXPENSES. Family incomes rise and fall over a lifetime. Learning management skills to adjust to such fluctuations has become increasingly important to many adults. For some, it means better budgeting of expenses in order to bring them under control. For others, it means better understanding of ways to spend more money.

The need for better budgeting can be triggered by many events. Perhaps the most common is retirement. It almost always means a loss of income, and adults may have to learn to cope with that problem.

> When my husband retired on a fixed income we found it very hard to manage the household budget, what with inflation and prices going up steadily. We had no way to get more money so we had to learn to trim expenses. That is why I'm taking this course in budgeting and managing household income.

As the population ages in the decade ahead, we can expect more and more adults to retire. Lower retirement incomes — which will be eroded by successive waves of inflation — will send more older adults back to school to learn how to manage on less.

The need for improved ways of spending money is often triggered by salary raises, more members of a family working, and increases in disposable incomes which may occur when mortgage payments are completed or children finish school.

> I had been working for the same company for five years without any salary raises, so I decided it was time to move on. I took another job with a competitive firm who offered me almost double my previous salary. At about the same time, my wife also got a raise. With the extra money in the family, we needed some help on how to best manage our finances. We wanted to make some investments, but didn't know how to go about it. Our bank was sponsoring a course in securities and investing at the Y, so we took it. It was quite helpful to learn about the objectives of investing, all the different types of investments, and the timing of the stock market. You really have to be money wise these days.

Rising salaries for both men and women, especially in the two-income family, may produce surplus incomes at some time in their lives. But the surplus won't last long unless it is used well; many adults will spend part of it on learning how to manage the rest of it.

CARING FOR OTHER FAMILY MEMBERS WHEN CHANGES OCCUR. Babies are born, teenagers become impossible, husbands have heart attacks, and wives become alcoholics — these and less dramatic changes punctuate family life. Many such problems require adults to learn how to get along with family members differently, or to care for them with new skills and attitudes.

The arrival of a child, especially a first child, often means learning new skills. While some adults acquire these skills without formal instruction, others want expert help.

> I just finished an early childhood course at the community college. I did it because we will be having our first child next month and I wanted to learn all about how to take care of the baby. The course covered infant care and child development during the first three years. I want to do what's best so I took the course.

A smaller number of adults of child-rearing age combined with a lower birth rate means that fewer adults will seek learning for this reason in the future. On the other hand, the skyrocketing number of husbands and wives who cannot get along together will lead to more learning or to still more divorces.

> You can't call it a course, really. But I'm learning or I'm trying to, and I by God hope she is. It's marriage counseling. Twice a week. Might as well be a course — and it'd cost a hell of a lot less if it were. Anyhow, I'm trying to learn that it's okay for her to work outside the house. That's really pretty easy. Hard part for me to learn is that it's supposed to be okay for me to do her work inside the house. It's learn it or Goodbye, Gladys, I suppose.

As we pointed out earlier, adults who cannot learn may fail to make their transitions successfully. Some adults are not learning to shift into new forms of marriage and will not succeed in being transformed spouses.

Changes in Leisure

Adult Americans spend 16 percent of their time in leisure activities. This is more time than they spend on anything else except their careers and family lives. In fact, adults spend half as much time on leisure activities as in family activities and almost 40 percent as much time at leisure as at work. Clearly, leisure is a major life area.

It follows that 13 percent of all their transitions are leisure transitions, requiring skills in sports, crafts, hobbies, and social activities for the sole purpose of making constructive use of free time. As people change their leisure activities, they often have to learn to succeed in new ones.

Leisure, we found, is an arena of achievement for many adults. They like to do their activities well. Thus we found adults busily learning tennis, skiing, dancing, party cookery, antiquing, genealogy, needlepoint, and gardening just for fun, or, more exactly, just to be good at having fun.

> I am trying gardening again. I tried it before and flopped, but now I am taking a gardening course and starting again. Last summer was the first summer I had spent at home. There was a change of staff in the university where I teach and my teaching load was reduced. Now I have the time to garden.
>
> . . .
>
> Until my little boy was 2, I stayed home with him. When he turned 2 and started nursery school, my older one was 5 and started kindergarten. I began to look around for things of interest to me other than baby or house. You stay home all the time with little kids and housework is just not enough. I had my freedom and I needed to use it. I had time then and I also needed to do something athletic for the sake of exercise. One of the things I latched onto was tennis. Everybody knew how to play tennis but me so I decided I had better learn how. I took tennis clinics with my husband. It was something we could do together, which was a nice change from staying home taking care of babies.

These two examples illustrate learning to take advantage of an increase in leisure — a leisure transition. In this first example, a reduction in the amount of time spent in paid employment, a condition that may increase for many Americans as the work week shortens, led to increased time for leisure. The second example suggests that similar families with fewer children in the nation's future will mean that more women will find their houses and their lives becoming empty when their first or second child goes off to school. Like our example, they will have the time and the need to learn something new for the long years ahead.

The triggering events in these two examples took place in the adult's work and family arenas. As explained earlier, the adults interviewed always placed the triggering event outside the leisure arena, always credited the learning to a change in another life area that in turn increased or decreased their leisure time. That is, adults learning to be more skillful at leisure — how to maintain their motorcycles, play tennis, bowl, read good books, dance the samba, or learn Spanish before touring South America — inevitably pointed to a row of falling dominos as triggering their learning. But the last domino was never in the leisure area. A typical chain of events went like this:

> When my husband died, I moved to Truth or Consequences and bought a condominium. There are many people my age in the complex. They are very active. They have formed an investment club and I joined just for the fun of it. The money doesn't matter to me, but the club meetings give me a chance to socialize with the other members while we're learning about investments and learning how to spend our money.

> .   .   .

> I was widowed at 25. I began taking lots of classes in ballroom dancing. I needed something to do, now that my husband was gone. I wanted to be a good dancer and meet lots of new people. For a single woman at my age in life, associating with other people was extremely important to me.

Many adults told us that the death of a family member — sometimes another adult, sometimes a child — had brought about significant changes in their lives. Losing a spouse through death at an early age or at any age, whether the spouse is male or female, is a highly significant life trigger for almost any adult. Making the successful transition to a new life often requires learning. Moreover, as some adults told us, learning is a reorienting experience that can help put the pieces of a life back together again.

Many adults explained that moving to a new location — sometimes a new house, a new neighborhood, a new city — triggered their learning of new leisure activities. Frequently, moving allowed them to learn something they had wanted to learn all along.

> I'm taking tennis lessons now. Before I took lessons, I started playing with my husband. Then, he started refusing to play with me because I couldn't play well. We ended up not talking to each other. But I couldn't do anything about it until we moved from an apartment to a house into a neighborhood where everybody

> played tennis. That had a lot to do with my taking lessons. Tennis is a very big thing where I live now. I knew I had to learn and I really enjoy it now.

With 20 percent of American families moving every year—10 percent to new cities—moving will continue to trigger learning for many adults.

Marriage often requires new skills: some are social skills that are practiced during leisure time.

> Neither one of us could dance very well when we got married. But we found out that the other young married couples were going out dancing. So we started taking disco dancing lessons so we could make new friends and go to the discos with them.

Some skills involve cooking, home decorating, home repair, or new skills in civic and community affairs.

Perhaps if we had interviewed more adults we might have found that 1 in 5,000 or 1 in 20,000 traced their learning to a triggering event in their leisure lives. It is not hard for us to imagine that if the only bowling alley in town burns down, many adults will make a transition to billiards or pinball and may have to learn to make three-cushion shots or add 30,000 points without setting off the tilt light. We also can imagine that with casino gambling becoming legal, many adults will spend less time in front of their television sets and more time learning whether to stand pat or ask for another card.

However, that is not how adults explained changes in their leisure learning. They consistently explained it as a shift in activities in some other life area, which in turn caused a shift in their leisure patterns, which in turn led them to learn.

Changes in Artistic Life

Some adults learn to perform or to produce as artists while others learn to appreciate the performances and productions of artists. Whatever the case, their learning encompasses dance, music, painting, and drama. These adults learn for a variety of reasons, most having to do with life changes they have made, are making, or want to make.

> When I got married, my parents gave me the piano that I had played as a child to put in my own home. I had not studied piano

since I was in high school because I did not have a piano of my own to practice on. But, when we moved into our own home and I stopped working, I put the piano in the living room and decided now was the time to start playing again. I arranged for private lessons and also am taking a course in music theory.

. . .

I began taking art classes about six months ago. A lot of changes occurred in my life at that time. I had just gotten my divorce, my daughter left home and it was just me and my son at home. So, I had an extra bedroom that I could fix up for my studio and more free time. I called up the studio in my neighborhood and found out that I could take classes during the day when my son was in school, and be at home when he came home. So, I decided to go out and do it.

Because adults engage in artistic activities primarily as a form of leisure, learning the arts is often triggered by an increase in leisure time, as in these two examples. We talked with one adult who said that retirement had given him the time to indulge a long-delayed interest in learning to paint in oils. We talked to an adult whose wife had died the year before; her death triggered his decision to join a group learning about architecture before touring the world's famous buildings. We talked to an adult whose recent disabling injury triggered a decision to learn enough to amass a personal collection of classical stereophonic tapes. It was evident that, even in the arts, learning usually means learning to cope with change.

Changes in Personal Health

Some adults learn to regain their health and some to maintain it. Most of the reasons related by the adults we interviewed could be classified into two categories: (1) recovering from personal injury or illness and (2) maintaining physical fitness.

Good health is the only desirable status. Thus, people learn for only two reasons: (1) to move into good health or (2) to avoid moving out of good health. That is, they learn because they have lost their health (a past transition), because they are losing it (a current transition), or because they are afraid they will lose it (an anticipated transition). In the first instance, the triggering event is becoming injured or becoming ill. In the second instance, the triggering event is something causing a person to realize that his or her health will deteriorate or will continue to deteriorate unless he or she learns new health habits.

RECOVERING FROM PERSONAL INJURY OR ILLNESS. Some adults explained that they had to learn their way back to good health.

> I'm learning how to walk again. After I fell down my front steps and broke my hip, the doctor put me into a hospital class taught by a physical therapist so I could learn to get around again. I've been going over to the hospital in my wheelchair an hour a day for the past three weeks. It's been a little slow for me — I'm 68 now — but I'll be up and around by my grandson's wedding this summer.

> . . .

> Just as soon as he figured out I had diabetes, my doctor wanted me to take lessons in how to give myself insulin injections and also lessons in what kind of diet I would have to follow from that point on. I finished the lessons last winter. Of course I'm taking the injections and sticking to the diet and feeling a lot better as a result.

While Americans are becoming healthier all the time — less injury because of the decline in manual labor, dangerous industrial practices, and warfare, as well as less illness because of better sanitation, better preventative medicine, and better nutrition — injury and illness still are common enough to cause some adults to learn.

MAINTAINING PHYSICAL FITNESS. Some adults have been swept up in the nation's current eagerness to maintain physical fitness. We talked to self-taught joggers, self-taught nutritionists, and self-taught organic gardeners. We also talked with people who were taking classes to keep themselves fit.

> I'm taking tennis lessons now to stay in shape. I met some new friends who wanted to play just for fun. My reasons were a little different. I wanted to keep in shape so I would feel good about myself. I had had two children and had just turned 30. I realized I wasn't a kid anymore. Somehow, even when I was 29 I was still

in my 20s and still thought of myself as a kid. But when I turned 30, I knew I would have to do something to keep myself in condition.

. . .

Since I was 17 I was a big beer drinker. But in 1973 I had a physical examination. My doctor said I had a high amount of triglycerides so knock off the carbohydrates. The next day I got a book on what carbohydrates were—I couldn't even spell the word. I found out that each can of beer has 15 grams of carbohydrates and dry wine has comparatively little. So I started drinking wine and cut way down on my beer consumption. After a while I began to appreciate the taste of good wine and said, "Too bad I can't get really good wine cheap." Then it dawned on me that you could get really good wine cheap if you had the time and patience to do it yourself. So I began reading books on wine making and got started. I've been making my own wine for five years now. I read a lot of books and talk to people that are also making wines to find out what they are doing so I don't make the same mistakes that they made. Now I'm aging some Zinfandels. I always make dry wine.

These cases illustrate two of the most common events triggering the decision to learn in order to maintain physical fitness or, to be more exact, to avoid losing it. The first is the realization that one is aging. Aging is continuous, of course, but the realization is discrete. Something happens to make a person realize that the years are slipping by and that fitness is slipping away: the arrival of a 30th birthday, a comment from a friend met after a few years of separation, or the wedding of one's child are the kinds of clear signals that can trigger the decision to learn how to stay healthy. The second is the realization that the poor health habits that had little effect on one's energy and appearance at a younger age are taking their toll at an older age. Such habits include eating too much, drinking too much, staying out too late, driving instead of walking, and watching television instead of playing ball. Again, something has to happen to make an adult acutely aware of the accumulating effects of these habits. Stepping on the scale for the first time in months, the inability to zip up last summer's dress, falling asleep at a party, or a glancing appraisal made by a friend absent for some years are the kinds of specific events that trigger the decision to start learning and, perhaps, to start losing.

Seventy-five percent of all adults now reach age 65 as compared with only 40 percent in 1900, and the life expectancy for those who reach 65 today is 16 more years. As the nation's population ages, more adults will need to learn to recover from personal injury or illness and/or to maintain physical fitness.

Changes in Religious Life

Some adults, particularly those who grew up in the South or who still live there, have an intensely personal relationship with God. Some told us that intensifying that relationship caused them to start learning more about religion or, more often, more about God's plan for their lives. Some adults explained that they had strengthened their relationship with God as a result of a direct, personal encounter, in some cases initiated by the adult and in some cases initiated by God.

> I was completely lost. I didn't have any purpose in life. I didn't know what I was doing. Then one day when I was at my lowest, God came to me. I knew from then on that God had a purpose in putting me here — things for me to accomplish, a way for me to live. That's when I started studying the Bible and I've been doing it ever since.
>
> . . .
>
> My church had always held retreats every summer. We would bring in an outstanding preacher from some other church and he would lead the retreat while our own minister was on vacation. I had gone to these retreats for years but two summers ago the preacher we brought in was so good. He prayed with me every day for God to take over my life. Nothing happened at first. But then, nearly at the end, God answered my prayers and came into my life. That's when I started adult Bible class at the church. Then I went to the retreat last summer and I have kept on.

Both these people underwent a major religious transition and they had to learn new values, new ways of relating to other human beings, and new ways of spending their time. The Bible was their curriculum; the minister their teacher.

Many other adults told us they were studying religion, usually studying the Bible, but we did not classify them as being in religious transition. These people fell into two groups: the first group was not in transition and the second was not in religious transition. The first group had been learning religion long before becoming adults—sometimes in childhood—and were not learning it now because of a transition. The second group of adults were learning about religion to help themselves through a transition in some other life area, but not a transition taking place within their religious lives. Most of those transitions involved family affairs or personal health. Typical examples were divorce, the severe illness or injury of a family member, the death of a family member, a severe personal injury or illness, extreme difficulty in raising teenagers, or other crises so severe that the adult turned to religion for support and guidance. (As we explained earlier, the subject of study is not necessarily related either to the transition or to the triggering event.)

Changes in Citizenship

Some adult learners attributed their learning to changes in their lives as citizens. Some learning was voluntary and some mandatory. Most of their reasons for learning could be classified into two areas: (1) becoming a citizen and (2) becoming a volunteer.

Becoming a citizen and becoming an active citizen are the two transitions represented here. Most Americans are citizens by birth, but hundreds of thousands more born in other countries have to learn before becoming United States citizens. But both native and naturalized citizens may have to learn to move from passive, nominal citizenship to active, responsible citizenship.

BECOMING A CITIZEN. Some adults explained that they were studying on their own or taking classes to learn English and the rudiments of American history and government in order to pass examinations and receive their official papers as naturalized citizens.

> I moved here with my family from Caracas three years ago and decided to take out my U.S. citizenship—my wife and I—about a year and a half later. I had learned a little English in high school in Venezuela, but not much, and my wife had never studied it. The local high school ran classes and both of us went for almost a year. At the end we took our examinations and both passed. We are very proud.

More and more adult immigrants are arriving on United States shores and many of them are deciding to stay. Immigration quotas have been raised; refugees continue to arrive from oppressed countries; temporary farm workers decide to become permanent residents; and illegal immigrants choose to make their status legitimate. All will need to learn their way into citizenship.

BECOMING A VOLUNTEER. Some adults told us that they had to learn to contribute to their communities as active citizens.

> I just finished taking a leadership course in Scouting. I am a Scout Master in the Boy Scouts. I felt I needed to know how they suggested to do things. My troop was not progressing the way I thought it should. I figured if I met people and got their ideas about how they run their troops and the way Scouting says you're supposed to run the troops, I would be a better Scout Master.
>
> · · ·
>
> The men couldn't see a female volunteer firefighter at first. But you have to take courses in Firemanic training to be a firefighter and I figured if I did well during the training, the other volunteers would accept me. I worked very hard in the courses—came early, stayed late, read all the materials, and really exerted myself in the training exercises to show how good I was. It worked. I'm a firefighter now and the men put up with me pretty well—most of them.

America has always been a land of volunteers. De Tocqueville observed it early in our history and today we have national, state, and local organizations of volunteers. Millions of Americans work in schools, hospitals, nursing homes, and social agencies; millions more work in political campaigns; as fire-fighters or auxiliary police officers; as coaches and directors; or in organizations for the young and the elderly in sports, theater, and music. Many of these voluntary activities require training in leadership skills, administrative organization, human relations, technical tasks, producing publications, or raising funds. Thus, becoming an adult volunteer often means becoming an adult learner.

As the tax dollar shrinks and publicly-supported programs struggle to maintain their services, they are likely to recruit more and more volunteers to assist or replace paid staff. Many of the new volunteers will become new learners.

HOW DO LEARNERS DIFFER?

Do people who learn because of life changes differ in personal characteristics from those who learn for other reasons? Are people who learn because of some change in their lives the younger, better educated, in higher paying jobs, or in other circumstances that cause their lives to change rapidly and thus require them to learn?

Moreover, among the 83 percent of adults who learn because of life changes, are there differences in personal characteristics that are related to the kinds of transitions or triggering events they experience? For example, do men, married people, or the employed differ from others in the status changes they must make and, thus, in what they need to learn? Or do professional workers or people with young children differ from other learners in the types of life events that cause them to decide to learn when they do?

The discussion here analyzes learners, transitions, and triggers according to nine demographic characteristics.

SEX. Men learn because of life changes rather than for other reasons slightly more often than women — 87 percent compared with 79 percent. It may be that men have about all they can do to keep up with the learning demands of the life changes they are undergoing while women have a little more time to learn things not required by a specific change in their lives (Table 20).

Twice as many men as women learn because of career changes. In contrast, about twice as many women as men learn because of transitions in each one of the other life areas. Those differences are about what one would expect, given the fact that twice as many men as women are employed (90 percent compared with 50 percent). It follows that men spend more time than women at work, while women spend more time than men in family, leisure, health, and other activities. More time in a life area presumably means more transitions in that life area requiring learning (Table 21).

The relationship between sex and triggering events is quite similar to that for sex and transitions, and thus is not discussed separately (Table 22).

AGE. Adults of all ages cite life changes rather than other reasons as the major causes of their learning. From age 25 through age 65, life changes explain about 85 percent of all learning with only minor differences from age to age. While there is a continuous decline in the proportion of adults who engage in learning as their years roll by — with an especially sharp drop in the early 40s and a long plateau sloping gradually downward thereafter — the shrinking proportion who do choose to learn are motivated by life changes just as often as their younger counterparts (Table 23).

Evidently, while getting a job may require learning for the younger adult, advancement may necessitate further learning for the older adult. While adjusting to marriage may cause a 25- to 35-year-old to learn, those in the middle years of life, 35 to 49 years of age, may need to learn something new to adjust to divorce, to children going off to school, or to college or work.

After age 65, life changes explain about 65 percent of all learning, still the majority but by a smaller margin. The primary reason for this drop, especially for men, is retirement from careers — a life area usually filled with changes requiring learning. But life slows down in other respects as well. There are fewer changes in the lives of the adult children, leisure patterns stabilize for older people, and the elderly change their homes less often. The effect of these stabilizations is that the elderly experience fewer life changes requiring learning.

What life areas require learning at what ages? Adults between the ages of 25 and 65 trace over half of their learning to career transitions. Far fewer adults learn because of other reasons such as family transitions (roughly 15 percent) or leisure transitions (roughly 10 percent). In sharp contrast, adults over age 65 trace most of their learning to leisure transitions (about 40 percent) and family transitions (about 20 percent) (Table 24).

This pattern can be explained easily. Learning for career purposes dominates adult lives, especially those of men, before retirement at age 65; leisure dominates adult lives after age 65 and there is more free time to engage in such activities as travel, hobbies, and crafts. This shift begins between the ages of 50 and 65, and intensifies after 65.

Along the same lines, we can see a definite increase in the study of the arts and religion after age 65, the former caused by adults turning to the arts as a form of leisure activity and the latter caused by adults becoming more and more conscious of their final years in life.

There are fewer contrasts among adults of varying ages in the types of events that trigger their decisions to learn. For both those under and over age 65, career and family triggers predominate, although not to the same degree. Of those 25 to 65 years of age, close to 60 percent cite career triggers; about half as many (35 percent) cite family triggers. On the other hand, those over 65 cite career and family triggers equally as often. Not surprisingly, health triggers as well as religious triggers increase with age — one indicative of declining physical conditions and the other of the need to intensify one's relationship with God (Table 25).

Evidently, what prompts most adult Americans to learn are changes in their work, be it for the purposes of getting, holding, or advancing in their jobs before age 65 or moving out of their jobs and into retirement after age 65. Regardless of their ages, events at home consistently provoke many adults to learn something new.

RACE. There are no differences among whites, blacks, and others in learning because of life changes as opposed to other reasons. Changes touch all of them and they all use learning as one means of coping (Table 26).

There are only small differences among the three groups — whites, blacks, and others — in the types of transitions that cause them to learn. Career transitions rank first for each group, with family and leisure transitions following at a considerable distance. The only differences worth noting are that whites and blacks learn in order to make leisure transitions more often than other populations, while other populations learn in order to make family transitions more often than blacks and whites. This presumably reflects a stronger family orientation on the part of the other populations (Table 27).

There are no appreciable differences among whites, blacks, and others in the kinds of events triggering learning. Events in the careers and families of all three groups accounted for virtually all learning (Table 28).

MARITAL STATUS. There are few differences among married, divorced/separated, widowed, and single/never-married adults in whether they learn for life changes rather than for other reasons. Divorced/separated adults most often learn because of life changes (86 percent of their learning) and the widowed least often learn because of life changes (74 percent of their learning). This small difference is understandable, given the fact that the married adult is more often younger, has a family, and is working (all of which mean life changes) in contrast to the widowed adult, who usually leads a life with fewer changes and is a bit more likely to choose learning as an activity because it is satisfying in itself, it keeps the adult mentally alert, and it provides regular socialization with other adults (Table 29).

Married people and divorced/separated people, as well as people who are single and have never been married, learn primarily because of changes in their careers, and, to a lesser extent, in their family lives. Widowed persons, on the other hand, learn in order to make better use of leisure and to cope with their family situations as often as they learn because of changes in their careers. Again, this reflects the advanced age of widowed persons, who spend as much time at leisure as at work. Single persons who have never been married, in contrast to others, spend little time learning to cope with family transitions, just as would be expected (Table 30).

Whereas career-related events trigger learning most often for single and married adults, the divorced/separated, not surprisingly, are influenced equally by career and family triggers, and the widowed most often by family triggers (Table 31).

AGE OF CHILDREN. Adults with children under 6 years of age learn because of life changes rather than for other reasons somewhat more often than other adults, and they learn more often because of life changes associated with their families. For example, adults with children under 6 are twice as likely to learn because of family transitions as adults without any children. The same pattern reveals itself in a weaker form among adults who have children over 6, with the relative influence of family changes on learning fading as children grow older (Tables 32, 33, and 34).

But the larger pattern is that having no children or having children of varying ages is not conclusive in determining whether an adult learns in order to deal with some life change, in determining the type of transition requiring learning, or in determining the life events that trigger learning. This may be because changes in one's life can be so critical that, regardless of one's responsibility for offspring, the need to learn in order to make a necessary transition — such as getting a job following a recent divorce, getting spiritual guidance following the death of a spouse, or acquiring house maintenance skills following the move to a new home — overrides learning because of changes brought about by having children.

EDUCATION. There are essentially no differences among adults of varying educational levels in the extent to which they cite life changes rather than other reasons for their learning. Whether they are high school dropouts or college graduates, all adults face changes in their daily lives that require them to learn new skills, new information, or new attitudes (Table 35).

However, there are differences in *what* adults learn. Those

who have had some college preparation as well as college graduates and those with advanced degrees more often learn for
career reasons (about 65 percent of those three groups) than
two-year college graduates, high school graduates, and high
school dropouts (about 45 percent of those three groups). The
former may be learning to keep up with or advance in their
professional/managerial jobs, whereas the latter—holding
nonprofessional, service-oriented, blue-collar jobs—do not
need to do so as often. Consequently they can spend propor-
tionately more time learning for family and leisure purposes
(Table 36).

Interestingly, there are fewer differences in the types of
events that trigger learning for the various groups. While
career triggers rank first and family triggers rank second for
all groups, a clear pattern exists: as one acquires more and
more education, learning is more and more likely to be triggered by career events (Table 37).

INCOME. As with educational level, income does not make a
difference in the degree to which life changes rather than
other reasons influence learning. Clearly, changes affect adults
at all income levels and learning is one way of coping with
those changes regardless of income (Table 38).

Income, however, is connected to the purposes of learning.
As incomes rise, adults learn more often for career reasons.
The sharpest contrast is between those with incomes under
$10,000 and those with incomes over $30,000. The first group
is more likely than the second to learn because of family and
leisure changes while the second group is more likely than the
first to learn because of career changes. The explanation presumably is that those with higher incomes spend more time
in career activities (Table 39).

This pattern is further documented in Table 40, which dis-
plays the relationship between income and events triggering
learning. Table 40 shows that persons who have incomes of
more than $30,000 stand apart from all other groups in the
degree to which career-related events require them to learn
at a given point in time—about 70 percent of their learning is
triggered by career events in contrast to an average of about
50 percent for all other groups. In contrast, those who earn the

least more often have their learning triggered by family events (twice as likely, in fact, as those who earn the most). Again, this presumably reflects the way in which those with different incomes spend their time (Table 40).

EMPLOYMENT STATUS. The employed, the unemployed, and students cite life changes as reasons for learning (perhaps because they are advancing in or seeking new jobs) more often than homemakers and retired persons, who have more time to learn for other reasons (Table 41).

The employed, students, and the unemployed learn to make career transitions while the homemakers and the retired learn to make leisure and family transitions (Table 42).

However, there are differences among students, the unemployed, and the employed. While students and the unemployed learn to acquire career skills, it is events in their family lives that trigger such learning. The employed, on the other hand, are making career transitions triggered by career events. The retired have their learning triggered by career events — most notably retirement — while homemakers, not surprisingly, have their learning triggered by family events (Table 43).

In short, if adults are working or are close to retirement, career triggers make them learn at certain points in time, in the first instance, to acquire job skills, and in the second, to acquire leisure skills. But if an adult is not employed (a student or one who is in-between jobs), he or she learns to get job skills but is stimulated to do so because of family events. Homemakers, however, tend to seek to succeed in family transitions triggered by family events.

OCCUPATION. Again, as with income and educational level, the occupational status of adult learners has nothing to do with whether life changes instead of other reasons cause their learning. Life changes touch adults in all occupations, and adults in all occupations use learning as one way of responding to those changes (Table 44).

Professionals and managers learn most often because of career transitions; sales/clerical workers, craftsmen, and service workers learn the second most often because of career transitions, while operators learn least often because of career transitions. That is, there is a positive relationship between occupational level and learning in order to acquire, advance in, or simply keep up with one's job. What is probably at work here is a matter of changing technology and changing government regulations, both of which affect professionals and managers. Such changes are less frequent and, of course, have less effect on the lives of other workers (Table 45).

The 1977 census showed that 25 percent of all jobs today are professional or managerial. The same census showed that professional jobs have doubled in the 20 years since 1958 and that managerial jobs have increased by almost 50 percent during the same period of time. As the professionalism of the nation's labor force continues to increase — and it seems inevitable that it will — more and more adult learning will be career oriented.

As would be expected, learning by professionals and managers is triggered by events in their career lives more often than for other workers. The same is true for craftsmen, due perhaps to the obsolescence or modification of their jobs because of rapidly changing technology. On the other hand, learning triggered by family events is more common among sales/ clerical workers, operators, and service workers. This is traceable partly to the fact that those occupations are filled disproportionately by women, for whom family triggers are usually more numerous than for men (Table 46).

Summary

Overall, adults' personal characteristics do not determine whether they will learn because of life changes more often than for other reasons. More than 80 percent of adults learn because their lives are changing. This holds true regardless of sex, age, race, marital status, age of children, education, income, employment status, or occupation.

However, among the 83 percent who learn because of life changes, there are clear differences in the personal characteristics of those who learn because of one kind of transition rather than another. For example, adults who learn because of career transitions differ somewhat from those who learn because of family transitions; those who learn because of leisure transitions differ from those who learn because of religious transitions; and so on. The differences can be summarized as follows:

- *Men learn more often than women because of career changes, while women learn more often than men because of family, leisure, or health transitions.*

- *Adults under age 65 learn chiefly because of career transitions, while adults over 65 learn chiefly because of leisure and family transitions.*

- *Adults who are single, married, or divorced learn mainly because of their careers, while widowed persons learn mainly because of their leisure and family activities.*

- *Adults who have attended four-year colleges learn most often for their careers, while adults who have attended high schools or two-year colleges learn most often for other reasons — primarily reasons regarding family and leisure activities.*

- *As incomes rise, adults learn more often for career reasons.*

- *Workers and students learn primarily to make career transitions, while homemakers and retired persons learn primarily to make leisure and family transitions.*

- *As occupational level rises, adults learn more often for career reasons.*

The pattern for the events triggering learning is quite similar and, thus, is not summarized here. For example, men learn more often than women because of career triggers, while women learn more often than men because of family, leisure, or health triggers.

WHAT AND WHERE DO ADULTS LEARN?

How many and what types of things do adults learn? Where do they learn them? For example, do they learn several things at one time or learn them serially? Do they study occupational topics more often than family topics? Do they fill community college classrooms but avoid four-year campuses?

Are how much, what, and where adults learn affected by whether they are in transition and by the type of transition? For example, do adults in transition learn *more* things at the same time than others? Does a career change automatically lead to the learning of new career skills, and does a family change automatically lead to the learning of new family skills? Does a career change require learning at a career site, and does a change in health require learning at a hospital?

NUMBER OF TOPICS. Well over half of the adult learners interviewed had learned two or more topics during the previous 12 months, and more than 20 percent had learned three or more things. Thus we know that half of the entire adult population is engaged in learning and half of the learners are engaged in fairly intensive study (Table 47).

Adults in transition are more often multiple learners (about 60 percent) than adults who are not in transition (about 45 percent). This is further evidence that adults learn chiefly to cope with life changes. Just as more of those in transition are learning, those who are in transition are learning more (Table 47).

Multiple learning is most common among adults who are in family, artistic, or leisure transitions. An impressive 80 percent learned two or more things in the past year. Our interpretation is that many of the people engaged in family transitions were homemakers, while many of those undergoing transitions in their artistic and leisure lives were retired. Both groups had the time to engage in several kinds of learning simultaneously. Multiple learning was less common for those undergoing career, religious, and citizenship transitions: only about 50 percent learned more than one topic last year. The adults least likely to undertake multiple learning were those undergoing health transitions: only about 25 percent learned more than one topic, probably because in many cases they were preoccupied with health matters and were less able to spend time in other life areas that might have required learning (Table 48).

TYPE OF TOPIC. The adults interviewed had learned an enormous variety of topics in the past year. There were some patterns: over 35 percent had learned topics related primarily to career preparation. (The 35 percent figure probably understates the learning of career-related topics. Adults taking academic courses, for example, are not included in the 35 percent, but adults frequently took them to meet career requirements.) Family life (including gardening and landscaping) accounted for about 15 percent of all adult learning, while fine arts and crafts accounted for about another 15 percent. Religion accounted for about 10 percent. The remainder of the adult learning was scattered over many other topics (Table 49).

Adults who were in transition learned occupational topics far more often than those who were not in transition (over 40 percent compared with about 15 percent). Conversely, adults not in transition were twice as likely as those in transition to study fine arts and crafts and four times as likely to study religion and ethics. As we have observed elsewhere, participation in the arts is a way of filling in leisure time for many adults, especially those not coping with some life transition. The study of religion and ethics, usually the study of the Bible, is often the habit of a lifetime rather than something undertaken to cope with a particular transition (Table 49).

As would be expected, adults undergoing a particular transition usually learned a topic related to that transition. For example, virtually all of the adults we interviewed who were undergoing a religious transition were coping with it by learning religion and ethics. The same pattern was evident for those undergoing a transition in their artistic lives: they were, almost without exception, studying fine arts and crafts. Most people experiencing a family transition were studying topics related to family living (including gardening and landscaping). Similarly, most of those who reported being in a health transition were learning new ways of spending their leisure time, such as engaging in new social activities or sports or keeping physically fit. Finally, just as would be expected, a clear majority of those reporting career transitions were learning occupational skills (Table 50).

LOCATION OF STUDY. More adults (28 percent) learned completely on their own than in any single kind of institution offering adult learning.[1] Significantly, the type of institution most likely to provide learning is an employer (17 percent). This can be explained by the fact that most adult learning is career related and many employers offer formal or informal instruction to help employees begin new jobs, improve in current jobs, or prepare for future promotions. Taken together, independent learning and learning supplied by employers account for almost half of all adult learning (Table 51).

The educational institution chosen by most adults as a place to learn is a four-year college or university (14 percent). Private instruction comes next, providing 12 percent of all adult learning. Then comes community/junior colleges, local school districts, and religious institutions such as local churches and synagogues.

---

1. Seventeen percent of these adults reported that *all* topics they studied during the past year were investigated independently.

Voluntary/community agencies or organizations and professional associations, none of which are organized primarily to provide adult instruction, account for a substantial 9 percent. Some other organizations, which are organized specifically to provide learning, although not necessarily to adults, supply 2 percent of learners each: correspondence schools, proprietary schools, and area vocational/technical institutes.

Educational institutions combined supply about 30 percent of all adult learning — about as much as adults undertake completely on their own. Learning for the remaining 40 percent is supplied by a cadre of private teachers and assorted institutions, agencies, and associations for whom adult education is only a secondary function.

Adults who learn because they are in some kind of transition learn in formal educational institutions (particularly collegiate institutions), at places of employment, and from professional associations more often than adult learners who are not in transition. Those not in transition, on the other hand, more often learn at religious institutions, from private instructors, and completely on their own. It appears from this that adults in transition prefer to learn in formal settings (Table 51).

As would be expected, the type of transition that an adult is undergoing has a lot to do with where the adult choses to learn. Roughly 25 percent of those in career transition learn at their places of employment while another 25 percent learn at four-year colleges and universities. This is an understandable split, given the fact that career transitions requiring learning are particularly common among highly educated persons with professional and managerial jobs (Table 52).

In sharp contrast, half of those undergoing family transitions learn completely on their own. Another 25 percent learn either through private instruction — sometimes from friends and relatives — and from religious institutions. As would be expected, 65 percent of those experiencing religious transitions learn to cope with them at religious institutions. However, a considerable number (about 43 percent) are studying religion completely on their own, usually through reading the Bible.

Adults going through health transitions are as likely to learn completely on their own (about 30 percent) as through voluntary/community agencies or organizations (about 30 percent). The remainder learn through extremely diverse means, including private lessons, courses taken in local school districts, and instruction offered by employers, churches, television stations, and newspapers.

Private instruction reaches its zenith (about 40 percent) among those undergoing artistic transitions, although they are just as likely to learn completely on their own. Roughly the same thing is true for those experiencing leisure transitions: about 30 percent learn through private instruction and 35 percent learn completely on their own. The only educational institutions providing a significant proportion of adult learning in art and leisure are local school districts (Table 52).

Summary

Most adult learners studied two or more topics last year. Those in transition more often were multiple learners, especially if they were in family, artistic, or leisure transitions rather than undergoing career, religious, citizenship, or health transitions.

More than half of all adult learners studied to cope with career transitions, most by learning career-related topics, as would be expected. Adults undergoing a particular transition usually learned a topic related to that transition.

About 30 percent of all adult learners learned completely on their own, about 30 percent learned at educational institutions, and the remaining 40 percent learned from people and at places for which adult education was only a secondary function. Adults in transition usually learned in formal educational institutions while others usually did not.

The type of transition an adult was undergoing affected the location that adult chose for learning. For example, about 50 percent of those in career transitions learned either at their places of employment or at four-year colleges and universities, while about 50 percent of those undergoing family transitions learned completely on their own. Of those experiencing religious transitions, 65 percent learned at religious institutions.

PART III: CONCLUSIONS AND IMPLICATIONS

The chapters in this section contain 18 major conclusions which serve to summarize the findings and suggest their general implications. The findings also suggest a series of specific action implications for the five populations the study was designed to help: (1) those who provide adult learning; (2) those who supply information and counseling to adult learners; (3) those who make public policy concerning adult learning; (4) those adults who are learning or who should be learning; and (5) those who study adult learning.

9

CONCLUSIONS

The findings are a rich source of information: some raise questions that remain unanswered; some answer questions that were not even asked; and some confirm the hypotheses with which we opened the study. Further research, of course, may confirm or disprove the findings. But the answers arising from this particular set of findings seem quite clear. They are summarized and supplemented by our interpretations here.

1. *We have indeed become a learning society.* The fact that half of the adult learners interviewed had studied at least two different topics in the past year is evidence of the intensity of adult interest in learning. The fact that adults had studied every imaginable topic — surgery and sales, sewing and sailing, Swahili and swine-breeding — is evidence of the breadth of adult interest in learning.

    Any nation in which half of all the adults, as well as virtually all of the children, learn something significant every year is without question a nation of learners.

2. *We have become a society in which adults learn everywhere.* It is not simply that some adult learning takes place outside formal education institutions; it is that most of it does.

This means that learning has become a characteristic of adult behavior, a pervasive and perhaps even a necessary aspect of adulthood in our society. It has become an activity without a fixed, predictable location — an activity that can and does take place anywhere. This means, in turn, that social institutions other than schools are gradually being redesigned to accommodate adult learning activities and, in many cases, to provide them.

3. *Many adults learn in formal educational institutions.* Approximately half of these learners attend four-year colleges; the other half divide themselves about equally between two-year colleges and local school districts. The remainder enroll in technical institutes, proprietary schools, correspondence schools, and every other kind of school available.

Almost all these educational institutions were originally designed for children and youth. Adults have slipped into the seats alongside their children and have become almost as numerous, greying the green campuses, making junior colleges familiar places to senior citizens, and preserving the jobs of thousands of professors while confronting them with a new breed of students. It seems inevitable that the new adult students will change the schools and colleges. Already, campuses have become quieter; could the influx of adult students be one of the reasons?

Sooner or later, eagerly or reluctantly, forced by circumstance or excited by opportunity, schools and colleges will have to accommodate this new clientele. Indeed, the process is already well under way.

4. *Many adults learn in institutions for which education is not the primary function.* Such institutions include the workplace, churches, prisons, libraries, museums, the armed forces, and others for which education has become a significant function.

All institutions that deal with adults are becoming, to some degree, teaching institutions. Their reasons undoubtedly are quite diverse. A company may teach to make its work force more productive; a library may teach to build adult traffic and boost circulation; and a church may teach to help its congregation deal with its teenagers. But in all cases, the teaching function improves the institutions' other functions and makes them more successful.

Noneducational institutions may be better places for adults to learn than educational institutions because their teaching is accessible, convenient, realistic, immediate, and applicable. If so, educational institutions can learn from them, and the first thing they might learn is to pattern their own offerings accordingly if they want to attract adults.

5. *There are virtually no kinds of voluntary organizations — associations of boat owners, minority advocacy groups, societies of senior citizens — which do not arrange some kind of instruction for their adult members.*

If de Tocqueville were to return to the United States today, he might well observe that Americans create organizations partly so that they can learn together. He probably would go on to note that as their members become more skillful, the organizations function better.

6. *Some adults take private lessons.* Private lessons include instruction in the fine arts, home arts, sports, and foreign languages.

Private lessons subtract the social factor from the learning formula and leave two adults: one who knows and another who wants to find out. The content may be trivial, but the learner is serious. It may be expensive but, in the eyes of the 12 percent who learn this way, it is worth it.

7. *Many adults learn completely on their own.* These adults proceed without regular teachers or formal instruction, buying or borrowing whatever books, tools, magazines, and supplies they need. They watch television, ask friends, observe relatives, help fellow workers, or use trial and error until they finally get it to grow or run or look right or make sense.

These adults demonstrate not only the independence but also the resourcefulness of adult learners. If schools and colleges want to understand their competition in the adult learning market, they have to realize that their greatest, toughest competitors are adults who learn on their own. What does the competition have to offer that the schools and colleges do not? Several factors give the individual adult learner a distinct advantage: Twenty-four-hour-a-day availability of instruction; variable-length lessons ranging from five minutes to five hours; a wide choice of locations, furniture, and lighting; food and drink on demand; and an instant end to boredom by closing a book or flipping a switch. What school or college can match — or should match it? Perhaps none. But that is one way to a larger share of the adult learning market.

8. *Adult learners differ in several respects from nonlearners.* Learners are younger, better-educated, wealthier, disproportionately white, employed (working at jobs in higher occupational categories), unmarried or married with a few young children, and more likely to live in urban areas or in the Pacific Coast states.

It is unfortunate that such clear cut differences exist between the adults who do and do not learn. Cannot adults of all types benefit from lifelong education? Why, for example, do the lesser-educated and the minorities not seek to learn as often as others? If we could answer this question, we would be better able to influence public policy to encourage them to do so.

9. *Most adults do not learn for the sheer pleasure of learning.* For most learning is not its own reward. Many enjoy the process of learning; some do not. Many enjoy knowing something new; some do not. But neither the process nor the possession is the reason most adults learn and neither, in itself, is enough to make most of them learn. Most learn because they want to use the knowledge.

While this finding is certain to disappoint most educators — who like to think that learning, both acquiring it and possessing it, are inherently rewarding apart from any use to which it might be put — they should understand that most adults use learning as the means to some other ends. The value of the learning lies in its utility. Educators will have to deal with that fact if they want to deal with adults.

10. *Adults learn in order to cope with some change in their lives.* Regardless of their demographic characteristics, almost all the adult learners interviewed pointed to their own changing circumstances as their reasons for learning. Further, adults who learn because of one kind of transition differ from those who learn because of another.

As we had hypothesized, it is being in transition from one status in life to another that causes most adults to learn. Adults learn what they need to know in order to be successful in their new status. Adults enter a learning experience in one status and expect to leave it in another. They will be disappointed if they go out exactly as they came in. The test of the learning is the success of the transition.

We believe that combining demographic characteristics and status change explains the correlation of demographic characteristics with adult learning. That is, younger, better-educated, wealthier whites working at responsible, demanding jobs and living in urban areas, particularly in the Pacific Coast states, are experiencing an extraordinary rate of change in their lives, and therefore are learning at an extraordinary pace.

Adults never outgrow their need to learn. Change touches the life of every adult, although it touches life at some points more often than at others and it touches some lives more often than others. Whenever change comes, early or late, and to whomever it comes, rich or poor, learning is one way of dealing with it. There are no types of adults, black or white, educated or not, blue collar or white collar, who do not use learning to accommodate the changes in their lives.

The learning a person undertakes is related to the transition he or she is undergoing. The transitions a person undergoes are related to his or her circumstances in life. Because those circumstances are measured by demographic indicators, the indicators correlate with the transitions, as shown in the following diagram.

These relationships explain, for example, why workers and students learn primarily to make career transitions, while homemakers, widows, and retired persons learn primarily to make family and leisure transitions. As demographic indica-

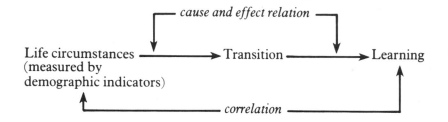

tors change to keep up with changes in life circumstances, they will continue to correlate with learning and the life transitions that cause them.

11. *Learning can precede, accompany, or follow life transitions.* Some of the adults interviewed were learning to cope with a change that had already taken place; others with a change still under way; and others with a change that lay ahead.

Learning can help an adult prepare for a future transition, deal with a current transition, or cope with life in a new status that he or she has already entered but cannot handle successfully.

Learning before a transition presumably is the best way. But adults cannot always plan their lives well enough to prepare for all changes ahead of time. Further, some institutional arrangements make it impossible. Military training, for example, is not available to most adults until they enter the armed forces. Company training is not available until an adult takes a job at the company. It is true, of course, that both military training and occupational training are scheduled immediately after an adult enlists or is hired. This suggests that the date of induction or hiring can be best understood as a triggering event, with the training preceding the adult's transition to actual job responsibilities.

12. *Transitions—and the learning needed to accomplish them—occur unevenly in the several areas of adult life.* More than half are career transitions; a smaller but substantial fraction are family or leisure transitions; a few are art, health, or religious transitions; almost none are citizenship transitions.

The major purpose for adult learning is to acquire occupational skills: The occupational motive outweighs all other motives combined.

There are several possible explanations for the predominance of career transitions. The first is that careers are more turbulent than other aspects of adult life; second, that career changes are more likely to require learning; third, that learning opportunities are more plentiful for career shifts; and fourth, that many adults think they can handle other kinds of life changes without learning anything new. But there is yet another explanation, simpler than any of these, which is probably the best. We present it next.

13. *The number of transitions in each life area corresponds exactly to the amount of time adults spend in each life area.* The adults interviewed spend about 80 percent of their time with their careers and families, for example, and trace about 80 percent of their learning to changes in their career and family lives.

We conclude from this that the best way to explain what adults learn is to point to how they spend their time. Occupational topics dominate adult learning because occupational matters dominate adult living. Changes occur in every aspect of adult life and adults have to learn to cope with all of them. An adult selects the learning needed for living. Thus, the adult learning pattern follows the adult living pattern. A high school student or a college student may wonder what some courses have to do with life, but an adult does not speculate. An adult knows exactly what the relationship is; otherwise, the adult will not attempt to learn.

We are talking here about the pattern of voluntary learning, which accounts for most adult learning. There is some involuntary adult learning, but it is difficult to force adults to study irrelevant topics. To do so ordinarily requires some type of compulsion, as in the military, in prison, as a condition of employment in a company, or as a course requirement for a degree in a college. Even with young people, mandating that they study irrelevant subjects works best if combined with compulsory school attendance. Relevancy, of course, is always in the eye of the beholder.

14. *Adults who learn because their lives are changing more often learn several things at once, more often learn career skills, and more often learn in formal educational institutions.* Conversely, those who learn for other reasons frequently learn informally about a single topic unrelated to careers.

We have several interpretations of this. One is that adults in transition have to juggle several problems at once and, thus, must learn more. Another interpretation is that learning is more urgent and more utilitarian for these adults. Another reason is that what they need to learn—usually about their careers—is so important that they seek out qualified teachers in schools and colleges. Finally, the new situations they are entering are rewarding enough, economically and otherwise, to merit the investment of time and money that formal schooling requires.

15. *Every adult who learned because of a transition pointed to a specific event in his or her life that signaled, precipitated, or triggered the transition and thus the learning.* Getting hired or getting fired, getting married or getting divorced, getting sick, getting elected, or moving to a new city were the kinds of events that told the adults it was time to learn.

For adults in transition, specific life events set the time on the learning clock: to know their life schedules is to know their learning schedules.

The need, the opportunity, and even the desire are not sufficient to cause most adults to learn at a particular point in time. There are millions of potential adult learners who need, want, and have the chance to learn. But it will take specific life events to convert most of them from latent learners into active learners. Decisions to learn may be pending for a long time, but the timing of their entry into the learning arena will be determined by particular events that permit—or force—them to enter it.

16. *Triggering events occur unevenly in the several arenas of adult life.* More than half are career triggers and almost all of the remainder are family triggers. Only a tiny fraction occur in other life areas, chiefly health.

The pattern is much like that for transitions. However, leisure disappears here as a category which leads us to conclude that while there are leisure transitions, there are no leisure events powerful enough to trigger life transitions and thus require learning to deal with them.

17. *The number of triggering events in each life area corresponds closely to the amount of time adults spend in each life area.* Adults spend about 80 percent of their time with their careers and families, and about 90 percent of the events triggering learning occur in their career and family lives.

The pattern again is much like that for transitions. The configuration of events triggering learning follows the configuration of all other life events. Career and family living account for most adult time and, thus, for most learning triggers.

18. *While the topic an adult chooses to learn is always related to the life transition requiring that learning, the topic is not always related to the event triggering the learning.*

We conclude that the kind of life change an adult is making — career, family, leisure — dictates the kind of learning the adult must accomplish — typing, cooking, tennis, etc. This is understandable enough. But the event triggering the decision to go to work as a typist may be a divorce; the event triggering the decision to learn to cook may be a heart attack; and the event triggering the decision to play tennis may be a job change.

The value of knowing what kinds of transitions cause adult learning lies in being able to predict *what* they will learn. The value of knowing what kinds of events trigger adult learning lies in being able to predict *when* they will learn.

10

IMPLICATIONS

Five separate sets of implications are drawn from the findings of this study, one set for each of the intended audiences: (1) those who provide adult learning; (2) those who supply information and counseling to adult learners; (3) those who make public policy concerning adult learning; (4) those adults who are learning or who should be learning; and (5) those who study adult learning. Although the sets of implications overlap to some degree, the differences are great enough to justify examining each set.

The implications will be of greatest interest to those concerned with the expansion of adult learning in their own institutions — and nationwide. They will be of least interest to those who are absorbed in educating younger students and who have no plans for serving adults.

In this chapter, we have cut the ropes that anchored our thinking to the findings. We have allowed our imaginations to float and we have been steered by our intuition. The implications are evocative rather than exhaustive. Each reader may see additional — or different — suggestions in the findings.

Implications for Providers

The educational providers, both formal educational institutions, such as two- and four-year colleges, technical institutes, and local school districts, and institutions whose primary function is not education, such as the workplace, voluntary associations, and the mass media, that want to serve the learning interests of adults can benefit in several ways from this study. The implications we have drawn can assist these institutions in identifying prospective clients, selecting marketing techniques, designing programs, and building relationships with other organizations. In this section we discuss some activities providers can carry out in each area.

Providers may find our list of suggested acitivities nontraditional, and, in some cases, may see them as being far-afield. Our intent is not necessarily that the suggestions be taken literally or implemented exactly; rather, we hope to encourage providers to stretch their imaginations in an attempt to envision new ways of identifying and attracting adult learners. The power of the findings is in enabling providers to locate people who are at a time of learning.

Identifying Prospective Clients

Providers may want to approach people who are in circumstances such as the following:

- Adults who are candidates for licenses usually have a considerable amount to learn in order to pass licensing examinations. These people include potential accountants, electricians, real estate brokers, and insurance agents. Providers may locate adults who are in the process of studying for examinations through sources such as employers, licensing bureaus, and professional associations.

- Parents who attend high school graduation ceremonies are often seeing their last child off to college. If the child is entering a private college with a high tuition, the family may be faced with the immediate need for a second income. The departure of a high school child, particularly if it is the last child, usually frees a woman for full-time work. Providers may locate such parents through the local school systems from which the students are graduating or through the post-secondary institutions which they will be attending.

- Providers can get from hospitals the names of mothers who had babies five years ago and who were over 35 years of age at the time. These children are now entering kindergarten. Inasmuch as the babies of mothers at age 35 are probably their last children, their entering kindergarten allows the mothers to undertake education, perhaps long-delayed education, now that they have the time and are somewhat free from family responsibilities.

- Families with a member who has suffered a serious injury or who has become disabled often need to learn how to care for the injured or ill member at home. Providers can contact the hospitals for the names of those families and the incidents which caused them to need such learning.

- Providers can identify people who are new in town through the Welcome Wagon or other newcomer services. Newcomers often need to make new friends, develop new patterns of leisure, or simply learn to fill in time until they become rooted in their new communities.

- People who retire at age 65 with a limited income need to learn how to manage their financial affairs so that they can successfully adjust to a more modest scale of living. Providers can locate these people through senior citizen's groups and housing complexes where the elderly reside, among other sources.

- Military personnel who retire after 20 years of service have a number of years of active life ahead. Many need or want to work and cannot transfer their military skills to civilian life. They need training and occupational skills just before or just after they leave the military to help them make successful transitions.

  The same is true for police departments, fire departments, and other municipal agencies which offer retirement after 20 or 25 years of service. Many people who retire from such agencies need and want to make transitions into other careers or into more active leisure pursuits. Many of them cannot do so unless they learn. Providers can locate persons preparing for or in their early months of retirement by contacting their current or former employers or their labor organizations.

- Many adults learn independently rather than attend formal classes. However, they may require certain assistance which providers can supply. These learners also may want to demonstrate what they have learned on their own and perhaps gain academic credit for it through examinations. This can be achieved either through tests created by providers themselves or through national examinations such as those prepared by the College Board through the College-Level Examination Program (CLEP). Providers can locate independent learners at libraries, bookstores, through the mass media, learner exchanges, and other settings where they seek help.

Selecting Marketing Techniques

Once providers have identified potential learners and are ready to market their services, they should:

- Recognize that adults have strategies other than learning to help them cope with life transitions. Such assistance includes turning to a personal friend or professional colleague, seeking the help of a counselor, turning to specialized agencies (e.g., employment offices, travel bureaus, recreation clubs), and so forth. Providers should show potential learners the special benefits and positive results their programs have had for others.

- Realize that they have a prime audience among adults already enrolled in their programs or the programs of other providers. The fact that most adults learn more than one topic at a time can be highlighted in the advertisements of any institution. Providers should emphasize the economy and advantages of simultaneous learning through multiple enrollments.

- Find out what the special incentives are for adults who learn from other providers. Providers can get this information easily through informal conversations, group meetings, observations in other settings, and through their own personal/professional insights. This analysis will yield good clues on how to appeal to the target audiences.

- Announce their programs through the publications of libraries, museums, churches, employers, voluntary associations, and other sources that reach potential learners efficiently.

- Segment the potential market in advertising programs directed to those most likely to enroll. For example, announce management training courses to young executives, retirement planning seminars to older executives.

- Recognize that adult learners are better educated, have better incomes, and hold better jobs; direct program announcements to them.

- Keep those who come in frequent contact with adults in transition up-to-date on current programs. This includes counseling staffs, personnel directors, lawyers and court officials, medical staffs, directors of community agencies, local school district employees, etc.

- Allocate advertising dollars to programs in life areas where adults spend most of their time — career and family.

Designing Programs

The findings give providers many leads regarding what adults in transition need to learn. This information is useful in designing programs that will attract and satisfy adults. An ideal program would be:

- Related to the seven life areas with the majority of programs devoted to careers, some in family and leisure, and few in art, health, religion, and citizenship. Providers that specialize in a single area should understand how this expands or restricts their potential market.

- Developed in light of the status changes adults need to make. Program planners must design their courses to help adults achieve their objectives — get a new job, raise a new child, or adapt to a new community.

- Differentiated to meet the needs of adults who vary according to level of education, income, occupation, and age.

- Complementary or superior to what other providers are offering. Adults have many options of where they can learn. Providers will be successful in attracting adults to the degree to which they keep their programs up-to-date, continuously raise and maintain high standards of performance, and get frequent evaluations from the learners themselves.

- Blueprinted by committees of those who know the most about the specific transitions adults are trying to make, such as employers, religious leaders, medical staff, and career counselors.

- Offered in different ways in order to match the various learning preferences of adults. This includes alternative schedules, methods, and locations.

- Equally effective in helping adults cope with transitions of the past, present, or future. Program planners should know the circumstances of the adults in their classes.

Building Relationships With Other Organizations

There are many ways providers can work with other organizations in their communities. Here are some examples of what can be done.

- Providers should assess the learning demands of their community jointly with other organizations. Information should be collected from adults themselves, employers, community agencies, and other organizations which offer or require training. The findings from such surveys can help providers predict what types of *adults* will need what sorts of *instruction* for what kinds of *purposes,* now and in the future.

- Providers can offer their programs under the auspices of other groups. For example, colleges of education can arrange with local school districts to train faculty in new curriculum approaches; graduate schools of business can arrange with professional associations to update members' competencies; YMCA's can arrange with senior citizen's groups to prepare members for leisure time activities; and correspondence schools can arrange with religious institutions to instruct members in ethics and values.

- Providers have much to gain from relationships they set up with employers who have both enormous requirements for training and the resources to support it. There are already a vast number of training programs operated by employers themselves. Generally, they do not wish to provide training, but they choose to do so because it is the least expensive arrangement they can make for supplying their own personnel with the skills they need. Companies most likely to need training for their personnel are those in highly technological, rapidly changing fields, and those under strict government regulation. Providers can approach such organizations and offer to take over some of their training activities. If providers can offer the training at less expense to the company, they have a good chance of seeing the company transfer the training program.

- Providers can improve their programs by using the staff, materials and equipment, and locations of other organizations. For example, a program in medical laboratory technology offered by a two-year college can be taught at a local hospital where the hospital staff and the special diagnostic tools available there can be included in the instruction.

- Providers should organize a community-wide adult learning council that can provide information about opportunities for learning in their area. This council can help providers decide what programs to continue, drop, modify, add, or offer jointly with other groups.

- Providers should initiate and maintain contacts with all types of organizations which represent or serve adults in their communities. There is practically no group which does not need to keep its staffs or employees — and those it serves — continuously up-to-date on new information and skills. From nursing homes, to the League of Women Voters, to hospitals, to professional groups, to Parent-Teacher Associations, to recreational clubs — all are potential sources of training ideas and trainees.

Implications for Information and Counseling Center Staffs

All agencies that offer information and/or counseling to adults about how to cope with their life circumstances are interested in locating adults they might serve. The previous suggestions to providers about how to locate prospective learners are equally appropriate for information and counseling centers. It is the adults in transition who are most likely to need assistance.

Information and counseling centers as well as providers can assume that the adults they want to serve will be at every ceremony celebrating a "marker event" in the life cycle (births, weddings, moves to new locations, graduations, retirement dinners, funerals — even 30th birthdays); in every institution with a temporary population (prisons, hospitals, schools, and the Army); and at every gateway in adult society (employment offices, marriage chapels, divorce courts, and funeral homes).

The findings suggest other areas that should interest center staffs. Some of them follow:

- Many adults in transition do not know that learning can help them succeed. Information and counseling centers need to understand that learning is one way of coping, and then explain it to adults as one promising option.

- Many adults do not know their own potential. Information and counseling centers can offer them an objective, honest, professional appraisal of what they might achieve.

- Many adults do not know what they have to learn in order to succeed, and in order to become what they can. Information and counseling centers ought to be lively catalogs of everything adults might learn, elaborately cross-referenced to how, when, and where that learning might be used.

- Many adults do not know where they can learn. Information and counseling centers should have a complete repertoire of places to recommend to clients. Staffs ought to be thoroughly grounded in the places where most adults learn: on their own, with employers, and at colleges and universities. In addition, staffs ought to know something about alternative locations: private lessons, library programs, museum tours and classes, church groups, correspondence courses, professional seminars, trade association clinics, labor union workshops, government programs, military training, vocational schools, television courses, travel-study groups — and many more.

- Many adults do not see benefits for themselves in learning in formal educational institutions. Information and counseling centers should examine the attractions of other providers so that they can advise adults of the special advantages of learning certain things in certain locations.

- Many adults do not choose providers on the basis of academic reputation but rather on how useful their learning would be. Information and counseling centers need to know which providers offer learning with the utility for particular clients with particular needs, and should recommend them regardless of their academic reputations.

- Some adults cannot find providers who offer suitable learning; other adults prefer to learn on their own, even if suitable providers are available. In both cases, information and counseling centers should guide these self-directed learners to support services such as directories on available materials, possible mentor relationships, and locations where the necessary space, equipment, and materials are available.

- Many adults cannot predict when and for what purposes they will need to learn. Information and counseling centers can assist clients by helping them forecast life events which will trigger the need to make a transition and, thus, the need to learn. With such guidance, adults will be able to plan and schedule their future learning.

- Many adults cannot make career transitions successfully through learning unless they have good information and effective counseling. Information and counseling centers need up-to-date information about the world of work and, in particular, predicted career patterns for the nation's workers. Then they can advise adults about what they need to learn, now or in the future, in order to meet their career goals.

- Many adults will not learn in life areas in which they spend little time and experience few transitions. Information and counseling centers should recognize that adults devote few hours to artistic, health, religious, and citizenship activities and, accordingly, will need to learn little in those areas. Center staffs should match their services to their clients' life schedules. Since most adults dedicate their time to their careers and families, center staffs must be prepared to deal with life changes and learning requirements in these two areas.

- Many adults are not deterred from learning because of their personal characteristics. Information and counseling centers should recognize that all types of adults experience change in their lives continuously and need information and/or counseling to assist them along the way. Center staffs must be trained to offer advice to all adults, regardless of their age, education level, income, or occupation.

- Many adults do not know that they might not even have to study—that they can earn high school diplomas or college credit simply by taking examinations to demonstrate what they have learned through experience. Information and counseling centers need to learn where and when such examinations are offered. They also can help clients obtain preparatory material and advise them on getting ready for taking such examinations.

- Many adults who are most in need of learning—the disadvantaged and the minorities—are least engaged in it. Information and counseling centers need to reach out actively if they want to serve these people since they are as unlikely to seek information and/or counseling as they are to seek learning itself.

Implications for Public Policymakers

Public policy for adult education is slowly beginning to resemble that for other segments of education: To provide readily accessible education at public expense without limiting or discouraging the provision of less accessible education at private expense. The effect has been to open almost all of traditional education to adults and to generate new forms of education designed to appeal mainly to adults. As a result, the range of adult learning opportunities is enormous—even though not every adult uses the available opportunities.

There are still some key policy differences. It is provocative to consider what might happen if the policies for adult education conformed to those for other segments of education. Such changes are contemplated here.

- *Adult education is usually viewed as open to all.* If it were recognized as closed to many who need it most—the disadvantaged and the minorities—then public policy could be changed in a serious attempt to open the door as wide for high school dropouts subsisting on $5,000 a year as it is for those holding advanced degrees earning $50,000 a year.

- *Adults are usually viewed as less able to learn than younger students, unlikely to major in specific subjects, and thus as not meriting the best instructors.* If adults were seen as being just as intelligent as younger students—as well as richer in experience, insight, and judgment—public policy could favor their getting the best faculty.

- *Adult education is usually viewed as a less serious, part-time enterprise which adults do not need as much as younger, full-time students.* If adult education were seen instead as a serious matter for adults—with their putting less time than younger, full-time students into recreation, socializing, spectator sports, and extra-curricular activities—then public policy could shift to favor adult education even if it is part-time.

- *Adult education is usually viewed as the low-prestige segment of campus offerings—especially in four-year institutions— with diluted academic standards and second-rate instruction in substandard facilities far from the campus library.* If adult education programs were seen instead as needing to offer quality instruction—although in nontraditional forms and times and places—then public policy could move to provide far better instructional arrangements for adults.

- *Adult education is usually seen as voluntary rather than com-*

pulsory as in elementary and secondary education. If adult education were recognized instead as being quite compulsory in some settings — for success of any kind in the military, for admission to advanced status in many professions, for promotion to better jobs in some agencies and organizations, for obtaining salary payments in CETA programs — then public policy could be changed to require education and training (or satisfactory performance) wherever it is needed in adult life.

- *Adult education is usually viewed as formal instruction in an institutional setting.* If it could be understood that adult *learning* takes place in many ways, formal and informal, institutional and independent, regular and occasional, teacher-taught and self-taught, then public policy might shift to encouraging and recognizing the demonstration of adult competency through the taking of examinations as well as through completing courses.

- *Adults are usually viewed as able to pay for their own education — unlike younger students.* If adults were seen as varying enormously in ability to pay — just the same as younger students — then public policy could choose income rather than age as the criterion for financial aid.

- *Adult education is usually viewed as conferring private rather than public benefits, aiding the individual adult more than the larger society, and thus as something the adult should pay for or contribute to.* If adult education were seen instead as an enterprise in the public interest — improving the labor force, strengthening family life, building physical health and physical fitness, guiding the constructive use of leisure time, encouraging religious and ethical development, enriching cultural life, making citizens better informed and more responsible — then local, state, and federal policy could converge to give adult education the same kind of financial support as elementary and secondary education.

- *Adult education is usually an administrative stepchild, tucked away in a corner of the educational bureaucracy and filed under "miscellaneous."* If it were recognized as the only growth sector in education in the 1980s as well as being as important as any other sector, it would be elevated to a high level in the new federal Department of Education. State education departments would then follow the federal lead, as they often do, and local school districts would do the same.

Implications for Adults

Adults themselves, both those who have and those who have not participated in learning as adults, should find the conclusions of this study useful in understanding and even in predicting how they may cope with future transitions in their lives. Here is some advice for them.

• Individual adults cannot control the biological, economic, and social factors that shape their lives. They do not live their lives on a plateau — their jobs change; their husbands or wives leave them; their children grow up and move away from home; and their health changes. Since they cannot prevent such changes, they must adapt to them. Adults should know that learning is one way of adapting.

• The accelerating pace of social change and the increasing rate of life transitions means that many adults have become lifelong learners. Adults need to understand this and to anticipate that they may need to undertake learning throughout their lives.

• Learning is a general-purpose solution to a variety of adult problems. Adults need to understand that it can be used to cope with changes in any life area — career, family, health, leisure, and others. At the same time, they need to remember that they will dedicate more time to their careers and families than to anything else and that the life changes they experience in those two areas, accordingly, will be the most numerous.

• Trouble in adulthood often can be defined as people being in situations without the knowledge, skills, and other tools needed to cope with those situations. Adults need to understand that they can learn their way out of commonplace kinds of trouble—whether it occurs as loss of job, loss of spouse, or loss of health. Learning provides a route to a new career, a different kind of family life, or renewed health.

- Learning can precede, accompany, or follow a transition. If adults understand this they can determine whether to learn before a transition occurs, by acquiring saleable skills before entering the job market; while the transition is occurring, by gaining a high school equivalency diploma as one acquires citizenship; or after a transition, by studying the Bible to gain a closer relationship with God after a serious illness or the death of a spouse.

- Specific events can give adults clues to when they need to learn. Adults need to know what these events are so they can schedule their learning. Such events include moving to a new community, re-entering the job market, taking a new volunteer job, creating a new job, having children enter school, and so on.

- The bigger the change in an adult's life, the greater the amount of learning needed. Adults need to understand that entering a new career requires more learning than entering a new job; moving across the country requires more learning than moving across the street; and adjusting to a heart attack requires more learning than adjusting to a broken leg.

- Adults can learn successfully in many different ways. They should know the optional ways of learning available and should match them to their specific purposes, choosing whatever will be most useful—classroom instruction, telecourses, correspondence courses, tutoring, or whatever is appropriate.

- Adults who engage in learning have disproportionately higher income levels, higher education levels, higher occupational levels, etc. Adults should understand that the cause-and-effect relationship between learning and being in better life circumstances has not been firmly established, but even so, they should consider whether they should try learning as a way of improving their life circumstances.

- As the pace of change in society and in adult life increases, adults may have increasing difficulty in knowing what, when, and how they need to learn to cope with those changes. They should understand that professional information and advice can be useful in making learning decisions.

Implications for Scholars

The findings leave many questions unanswered, questions suitable for future investigation. The College Board expects to pursue some of these areas. However, it is also likely that federal and state agencies as well as non-profit organizations may support scholarly inquiry and research into these questions.

Some of the questions that seem to be of primary importance are:

- Presumably all adults are in transition. Why do some adults choose learning as a means to succeed, while others do not? Do other adults fail at their transitions? Or do they have alternative ways of coping that make it unnecessary for them to learn?

- Is the attempt to distinguish between life transitions and specific triggering events worthwhile? Are there better or clearer concepts with greater explanatory power?

- What is the anatomy of career entry, progression, and exit as it relates to learning? Does it work in the same way for women as for men? Will the growth of learning as a means of career re-entry for women be followed by a similar growth as a means of career advancement? As technology envelops more and more occupational fields, will it continue to precipitate learning or will the labor force develop sufficiently transferable technical skills so that new learning is not necessary?

- Why do the advantaged learn more often than the disadvantaged? Do the disadvantaged not have as many transitions, or do they not see school as useful in making those transitions? Do they not know which school programs exist that might help them, or are they unable to take advantage of existing programs because of social, economic, educational, or geographic barriers?

- Is there some optimum match between a given type of transition and a given provider of learning? Are employers the best providers for those in career transition, for example, or churches best for those in religious transition? Or are all providers equally suitable as long as the learning itself matches the transition?

- What kinds of learning resources and psychological support, if any, are most helpful to adults who learn on their own?

- Is there a better classification system for transitions than the set used here: career, family, leisure, health, art, religion, and citizenship?

- Is there a substantial class of lifelong learners who learn because of the sheer pleasure of the process or because of the sheer satisfaction of possessing knowledge? What are their distinguishing characteristics? What, how, when, from whom, and with whom are they most likely to learn?

- Adult participation in learning is increasing, but at a slower rate than in earlier years. If social and economic changes are taking place at an ever-increasing rate, why isn't adult participation in learning taking place at an ever-increasing rate?

- What are the limits to the growth of adult education, if any? Is there some maximum proportion of adults in the society who can be engaged in learning at the same time? Is there some maximum proportion of all adult time that can be constructively dedicated to learning rather than to other activities needed to maintain the society?

REFERENCES

Anderson, Richard, and Darkenwald, Gordon. *Participation and Persistence in American Adult Education.* New York: College Entrance Examination Board, 1979.

Arbeiter, S., Schmerbeck, F. A., Aslanian, C. B., and Brickell, H. M. *40 Million Americans in Career Transition: The Need for Information.* New York: College Entrance Examination Board, 1976.

Brickell, Henry M. *A Study of the Tuition Refund Plan at Mack Trucks, Incorporated, Hagerstown, Maryland.* New York: College Entrance Examination Board, 1979.

Carp, A., Peterson, R. E., and Roelfs, P. J. "Adult Learning Interests and Experiences." In *Planning Non-Traditional Programs.* Ed. K. P. Cross, J. Valley, and Associates. San Francisco: Jossey-Bass, 1974.

Cohen-Rosenthal, Edward. "Lifelong Learning—For Some of the People," *Change,* August 1977.

Cross, K. P. "Adult Learners: Characteristics, Needs, and Interests." In *Toward Lifelong Learning in America: A Sourcebook for Planners.* R. E. Peterson and Associates. San Francisco: Jossey-Bass, 1979.

Cross, K. P. "A Critical Review of State and National Studies of the Needs and Interests of Adult Learners." In *Conference Report: Adult Learning Needs and the Demand for Lifelong Learning.* Ed.

Charles B. Stalford. Washington, D.C.: National Institute of Education, U.S. Department of Health, Education, and Welfare, 1978a.

Cross, K. P. *The Missing Link: Connecting Adult Learners to Learning Resources.* New York: College Entrance Examination Board, 1978b.

Gallup, George H. "The 10th Annual Gallup Poll of the Public's Attitudes Toward the Public Schools," *Phi Delta Kappa,* September 1978.

Ginzberg, Eli. "The Professionalization of the U.S. Labor Force," *Scientific American,* 240:3 (March 1979).

Gould, Roger L. *Transformations.* New York: Simon and Schuster, 1978.

Guzzard, Walter, Jr. "Demography's Good News for the Eighties," *Fortune,* November 1979.

Houle, Cyril O. *The Inquiring Mind.* Madison, Wis.: University of Wisconsin Press, 1961.

Johansen, Robert, and Samuel, Patricia A. *Future Societal Developments and Postsecondary Education.* Menlo Park, Calif.: Institute for the Future, March 1977.

Johnstone, John W. S., and Rivera, Ramon J. *Volunteers for Learning.* Chicago: Adine, 1965.

Kidd, J. R. *How Adults Learn.* New York: Association Press, 1977.

Kimmel, Ernest, Harwood, Beatrice, and Driver, Martha. *Education for Adults: Who Are They? What Do They Want? What Is Available for Them?* Princeton, N.J.: Educational Testing Service, 1976.

Knox, Alan B. *Adult Development and Learning.* San Francisco: Jossey-Bass, 1977.

Levinson, Daniel J. *The Seasons of a Man's Life.* New York: Alfred A. Knopf, 1978.

Lewin, Kurt. *Resolving Social Conflicts.* New York: Harper & Brothers, 1948.

Lowenthal, Marjorie F., Thurnher, Majda, and Chiriboga, David. *Four Stages of Life.* San Francisco: Jossey-Bass, 1975.

Morstain, Barry R., and Smart, John C. "A Motivational Typology of Adult Learners," *Journal of Higher Education,* 48:6 (November/December, 1977): 665-679.

Moses, Stanley. *The Learning Force: An Approach to the Politics of Education.* Syracuse, N.Y.: Educational Policy Research Center, 1970.

National Center for Education Statistics. *Participation in Adult Education, Final Report, 1975.* Washington, D.C.: National Center for Education Statistics, U.S. Department of Health, Education, and Welfare, 1975.

National Committee on Careers for Older Americans. *Older Americans: An Untapped Resource.* New York: Academy for Educational Development, 1979.

Neugarten, Bernice L., Ed. *Middle Age and Aging.* Chicago: University of Chicago Press, 1968.

O'Keefe, Michael. *The Adult, Education, and Public Policy.* Cambridge, Mass.: Aspen Institute for Humanistics Studies, 1977.

Penland, Patrick R. *Individual Self-Planned Learning in America.* Washington, D.C.: U.S. Department of Health, Education, and Welfare, 1977.

Pifer, Alan. "Women Working: Toward a New Society." In *Annual Report of the Carnegie Corporation.* New York: Carnegie Corporation, 1976.

Schlossberg, Nancy K. *A Model for Analyzing Human Adaptation to Transition.* College Park, Md., 1979. (Mimeographed.)

Sheehy, Gail. *Passages: Predictable Crises of Adult Life.* New York: Bantam Books, 1976.

Tolman, E. C. *Purposive Behavior in Animals and Men.* New York: Appleton-Century-Crofts, 1932.

Tough, Allen. *The Adult's Learning Project.* Toronto: Ontario Institute for Studies in Education, 1971.

Tough, Allen. "Major Learning Efforts: Recent Research and Future Directions," *Adult Education,* 28:4 (Summer 1978).

U.S. News and World Report. "Challenges of the '80's," *U.S. News and World Report,* October 15, 1979.

Vaillant, George E. *Adaptation to Life.* Boston: Little, Brown, and Company, 1977.

APPENDICES

APPENDIX A: TABLES

Table 1: Learning Now or in Past 12 Months

| Learning | Adults in Study | | Study Results Extrapolated to Nation |
	Number	Percent	
Yes	744	49	62 million
No	775	51	64 million
Total	1519	100	126 million

Table 2: Age

Age	Learners (N = 744)	Nonlearners (N = 775)	Total (N = 1,519)
25 – 29	20%	11%	16%
30 – 34	17	9	13
35 – 39	13	9	12
40 – 44	8	7	8
45 – 49	8	9	9
50 – 54	7	11	9
55 – 59	6	10	9
60 – 64	5	8	6
65 – 69	5	10	6
70 +	4	13	8
Refused	3	3	3

Table 3: Education

Education	Learners (N = 744)	Nonlearners (N = 775)	Total (N = 1,519)
8 years of school or less	4%	18%	11%
1-3 years of high school	8	16	12
High school diploma	33	37	35
Business or trade school	5	3	4
Some college	20	12	16
4-year college degree	13	7	10
Graduate or professional school	17	7	12

Table 4: Family Income

Family Income	Learners (N = 744)	Nonlearners (N = 775)	Total (N = 1,519)
Under $5,000	7%	20%	14%
$ 5,000 – $ 9,999	11	12	11
$10,000 – $14,999	18	15	16
$15,000 – $19,999	15	12	14
$20,000 – $24,999	12	8	10
$25,000 – $29,999	9	4	6
$30,000 – $34,999	5	3	4
$35,000 – $49,999	4	2	3
$50,000 +	4	2	3
Don't know	4	6	5
Refused	11	16	13

Table 5: Employment Status

Employment Status	Learners (N = 744)	Nonlearners (N = 775)	Total (N = 1,519)
Employed (Net)	71%	54%	62%
Full-time	64	49	56
Part-time	7	4	6
Retired	9	22	16
Homemaker	15	18	16
Student	2	0*	1
Unemployed	3	6	4

* Less than one-half of 1 percent.

Table 6: Occupation

Occupation	Learners (N = 528)	Nonlearners (N = 414)	Total (N = 942)
Professional, technical	28%	12%	21%
Managers, proprietors, and officials	25	20	23
Salesworkers, clerical	22	20	21
Craftsmen	12	22	16
Operators	4	12	7
Laborers, except farm	2	2	2
Farmers, farm workers	0	1	1
Service workers	8	10	9

Table 7: Occupational Area

Occupational Area	Learners (N = 528)	Nonlearners (N = 414)	Total (N = 942)
Agriculture/forestry and fisheries	2%	3%	3%
Mining	1	2	1
Construction	4	8	6
Manufacturing of durable goods	12	12	12
Manufacturing of nondurable goods	6	10	8
Manufacturing, unspecified	1	1	1
Transportation	2	5	3
Communications	2	1	1
Utilities/sanitary services	2	2	2
Wholesale trade	0	3	2
Retail trade	11	15	13
Finance/insurance/ real estate	6	5	6
Business and repair services	6	5	5
Personal services	5	4	4
Entertainment/recreation services	1	1	1
Professional and related services	30	18	25
Public administration	9	5	7
All other	0	—	—

Table 8: Marital Status

Marital Status	Learners (N=744)	Nonlearners (N=775)	Total (N=1,519)
Married	67%	64%	66%
Divorced	10	7	9
Widowed	9	16	13
Separated	2	3	2
Never married/ single	12	9	11

Table 9: Age of Children of Female Respondents

Age of Children	Children of Learners (N=792)	Children of Nonlearners (N=826)	Total (N=1,618)
2 or under	3%	2%	2%
3−4	5	2	3
5−8	9	5	7
9−12	12	8	9
13−17	18	11	14
18−21	14	13	14
22−24	8	10	8
25+	37	48	40

Table 10: Number of Children

Number of Children	Learners (N=744)	Nonlearners (N=775)	Total (N=1,519)
None	23%	21%	22%
1	16	17	16
2	26	25	25
3	18	16	17
4	10	9	10
5 or more	5	13	10

Table 11: Race

Race	Learners (N=744)	Nonlearners (N=775)	Total (N=1,519)
Hispanic	2%	2%	2%
Black	8	13	11
White	87	83	85
Other	2	1	2

Table 12: Population of City/Town

Population	Learners (N=744)	Nonlearners (N=775)	Total (N=1,519)
Under 2,500	13%	18%	15%
2,500 – 9,999	21	21	21
10,000 – 49,999	22	22	22
50,000 – 249,999	20	18	19
250,000 and over	24	22	23

Table 13: Geographical Regions

Geographical Region	Learners (N=744)	Nonlearners (N=775)	Total (N=1,519)
New England	5%	5%	5%
Middle Atlantic	18	17	18
South Atlantic	14	17	16
East South Central	7	7	7
West South Central	9	10	10
East North Central	20	19	20
West North Central	7	9	8
Mountain	4	4	4
Pacific	16	12	14

Table 14: Sex

Sex	Learners (N=744)	Nonlearners (N=775)	Total (N=1,519)
Male	48%	50%	49%
Female	52	50	51

Table 15: Number of Persons in Household 25 Years of Age or Older

Number of Persons	Learners (N=744)	Nonlearners (N=775)	Total (N=1,519)
1	30%	30%	30%
2	64	62	63
3	4	6	5
4	1	1	1
5	0	0	0
6 or more	0	0	0

Table 16: Reasons for Learning

Type of Reason	Learners (N = 744)
Life changes*	83%
Other	17

* Life changes include both "life transitions" and "triggering events." Every adult in transition named a triggering event as signaling the transition.

Table 17: Transitions Requiring Learning

Life Area of Transition	Learners in Transition* (N = 616)
Career	56%
Family	16
Leisure	13
Art	5
Health	5
Religion	4
Citizenship	1

* Percent of reasons given by the 83 percent who gave life changes as their reasons for learning; for example, 56 percent of the 83 percent who cited life changes named transitions in their careers.

Table 18: Triggers for Learning

Life Area of Trigger	Learners in Transition* (N = 616)
Career	56%
Family	36
Health	4
Religion	2
Citizenship	1
Art	0
Leisure	0

* Percent of reasons given by the 83 percent who gave life changes as their reasons for learning; for example, 36 percent of the 83 percent who cited life changes named triggers in their family lives.

Table 19: Transitions, Triggers, and Life Schedules

Life Area of Transitions and Triggers	Transitions* (N = 616)	Triggers* (N = 616)	Time Spent in Life Area
Career	56%	56%	44%
Family	16	36	34
Leisure	13	0	16
Art	5	0	0
Health	5	4	2
Religion	4	2	3
Citizenship	1	1	0

* Percent of reasons given by the 83 percent who gave life changes as their reasons for learning; for example, 56 percent of the 83 percent who cited life changes named transitions in their careers.

Table 20: Reasons for Learning by Sex

Type of Reason	Male (N = 355)	Female (N = 389)
Life changes*	87%	79%
Other	13	21

* Life changes include both "life transitions" and "triggering events." Every adult in transition named a triggering event as signaling the transition.

Table 21: Transitions Requiring Learning by Sex

Life Area of Transition	Male (N = 310)	Female (N = 306)
Career	71%	42%
Family	10	21
Health	3	7
Religion	3	5
Leisure	10	16
Art	3	7
Citizenship	1	2

Table 22: Triggers for Learning by Sex

Life Area of Trigger	Male (N=310)	Female (N=306)
Career	73%	39%
Family	20	52
Health	3	6
Religion	3	2
Leisure	0	0
Art	0	0
Citizenship	0	2

Table 23: Reasons for Learning by Age

Type of Reason	25−35 (N=274)	36−49 (N=222)	50−65 (N=163)	Over 65 (N=63)
Life changes	87%	83%	83%	63%
Other	12	17	17	37

Table 24: Transitions Requiring Learning by Age

Life Area of Transition	25−35 (N=240)	36−49 (N=185)	50−65 (N=135)	Over 65 (N=40)
Career	61%	63%	54%	2%
Family	17	14	16	22
Health	4	6	4	5
Religion	3	3	4	13
Leisure	8	9	17	40
Art	6	3	4	13
Citizenship	1	1	1	5

Table 25: Triggers for Learning by Age

Life Area of Trigger	25−35 (N=240)	36−49 (N=185)	50−65 (N=135)	Over 65 (N=40)
Career	58%	57%	57%	40%
Family	38	35	33	43
Health	2	5	7	8
Religion	1	2	3	8
Leisure	0	0	0	0
Art	0	0	0	0
Citizenship	1	1	0	3

Table 26: Reasons for Learning by Race

Type of Reason	White (N = 645)	Black (N = 62)	Other (N = 27)
Life changes	83%	84%	89%
Other	17	16	11

Table 27: Transitions Requiring Learning by Race

Life Area of Transition	White (N = 532)	Black (N = 52)	Other (N = 24)
Career	56%	62%	55%
Family	16	12	25
Health	5	4	4
Religion	4	2	4
Leisure	13	15	8
Art	5	6	4
Citizenship	2	0	0

Table 28: Triggers for Learning by Race

Life Area of Trigger	White (N = 532)	Black (N = 52)	Other (N = 24)
Career	56%	58%	50%
Family	36	37	42
Health	5	4	4
Religion	2	2	4
Leisure	0	0	0
Art	0	0	0
Citizenship	1	0	0

Table 29: Reasons for Learning by Marital Status

Type of Reason	Married (N = 503)	Divorced/ Separated (N = 91)	Widowed (N = 65)	Single/ Never Married (N = 85)
Life changes	84%	86%	74%	80%
Other	16	14	26	20

Table 30: Transitions Requiring Learning by Marital Status

Life Area of Transition	Married (N=423)	Divorced/ Separated (N=78)	Widowed (N=48)	Single/ Never Married (N=67)
Career	59%	64%	25%	51%
Family	16	17	21	9
Health	5	5	4	4
Religion	3	4	6	6
Leisure	11	6	29	21
Art	5	1	13	7
Citizenship	1	3	2	1

Table 31: Triggers for Learning by Marital Status

Life Area of Trigger	Married (N=423)	Divorced/ Separated (N=78)	Widowed (N=48)	Single/ Never Married (N=67)
Career	58%	47%	40%	67%
Family	35	45	56	22
Health	5	4	2	6
Religion	2	1	2	5
Leisure	0	0	0	0
Art	0	0	0	0
Citizenship	1	3	0	0

Table 32: Reasons for Learning by Age of Children

Type of Reason	None (N=169)	Under 6 (N=153)	6–17 (N=286)	18 and older (N=296)
Life changes	83%	90%	84%	81%
Other	17	10	16	19

Table 33: Transitions Requiring Learning by Age of Children

Life Area of Transition	None (N−139)	Under 6 (N−137)	6–17 (N=241)	18 and older (N=240)
Career	59%	58%	60%	53%
Family	11	22	17	14
Health	6	5	5	4
Religion	4	3	3	4
Leisure	14	8	10	17
Art	6	4	5	6
Citizenship	2	1	1	1

Table 34: Triggers for Learning by Age of Children

Life Area of Trigger	None (N=139)	Under 6 (N=137)	6–17 (N=241)	18 and older (N=240)
Career	63%	58%	56%	53%
Family	26	39	36	38
Health	7	3	4	5
Religion	4	0	2	3
Leisure	0	0	0	0
Art	0	0	0	0
Citizenship	1	1	1	1

Table 35: Reasons for Learning by Education

Type of Reason	Less Than High School Graduate (N=92)	High School Graduate (N=243)	Some College (N=135)	2-Year College Graduate (N=53)	College Graduate (N=95)	Graduate and Professional School (N=125)
Life changes	79%	82%	84%	87%	83%	83%
Other	21	18	16	13	17	17

Table 36: Transitions Requiring Learning by Education

Life Area of Transition	Less Than High School Graduate (N=73)	High School Graduate (N=200)	Some College (N=113)	2-Year College Graduate (N=46)	College Graduate (N=79)	Graduate and Professional School (N=104)
Career	42%	51%	69%	48%	60%	63%
Family	21	19	9	18	11	16
Health	4	6	3	2	5	5
Religion	8	4	3	2	4	1
Leisure	19	12	10	16	14	11
Art	4	4	6	9	6	4
Citizenship	1	2	1	5	0	0

Table 37: Triggers for Learning by Education

Life Area of Trigger	Less Than High School Graduate (N=73)	High School Graduate (N=200)	Some College (N=113)	2-Year College Graduate (N=46)	College Graduate (N=79)	Graduate and Professional School (N=104)
Career	47%	51%	58%	63%	61%	64%
Family	40	41	35	30	30	33
Health	4	5	4	4	6	4
Religion	7	2	2	2	3	0
Leisure	0	0	0	0	0	0
Art	0	0	0	0	0	0
Citizenship	3	2	1	0	0	0

Table 38: Reasons for Learning by Income

Type of Reason	Under $10,000 (N=135)	$10,000 – $19,999 (N=244)	$20,000 – $29,999 (N=162)	$30,000 and Over (N=92)
Life changes	84%	83%	86%	91%
Other	16	17	14	9

Table 39: Transitions Requiring Learning by Income

Life Area of Transition	Under $10,000 (N=113)	$10,000 – $19,999 (N=202)	$20,000 – $29,999 (N=139)	$30,000 and Over (N=84)
Career	44%	54%	64%	71%
Family	14	21	14	7
Health	4	5	2	4
Religion	9	3	3	0
Leisure	18	11	11	11
Art	8	4	6	7
Citizenship	3	1	1	0

Table 40: Triggers for Learning by Income

Life Area of Trigger	Under $10,000 (N=113)	$10,000– $19,999 (N=202)	$20,000– $29,999 (N=139)	$30,000 and Over (N=84)
Career	43%	57%	56%	71%
Family	44	36	38	23
Health	5	4	4	6
Religion	5	2	2	0
Leisure	0	0	0	0
Art	0	0	0	0
Citizenship	2	1	0	0

Table 41: Reasons for Learning by Employment Status

Type of Reason	Employed (N=524)	Student (N=17)	Homemaker (N=110)	Retired (N=70)	Unemployed (N=22)
Life changes	85%	100%	72%	74%	91%
Other	15	0	28	26	9

Table 42: Transitions Requiring Learning by Employment Status

Life Area of Transition	Employed (N=447)	Student (N=17)	Homemaker (N=79)	Retired (N=52)	Unemployed (N=20)
Career	69%	76%	13%	6%	50%
Family	12	6	37	21	25
Health	4	0	9	8	10
Religion	2	6	11	6	0
Leisure	8	6	20	46	5
Art	4	6	8	8	5
Citizenship	0	0	3	6	5

Table 43: Triggers for Learning by Employment Status

Life Area of Trigger	Employed (N=447)	Student (N=17)	Homemaker (N=79)	Retired (N=52)	Unemployed (N=20)
Career	66%	35%	18%	46%	30%
Family	29	59	68	37	60
Health	3	0	8	10	10
Religion	2	6	4	6	0
Leisure	0	0	0	0	0
Art	0	0	0	0	0
Citizenship	1	0	3	2	0

Table 44: Reasons for Learning by Occupation

Type of Reason	Professional, Technical (N=149)	Managers, Officials (N=128)	Salesworkers, Clerical (N=112)	Craftsmen (N=61)	Operators (N=22)	Laborers and Farm Workers (N=11)	Service Workers (N=40)
Life changes	86%	89%	82%	84%	86%	73%	85%
Other	14	11	18	16	14	27	15

Table 45: Transitions Requiring Learning by Occupation

Life Area of Transition	Professional, Technical (N=128)	Managers, Officials (N=114)	Salesworkers, Clerical (N=92)	Craftsmen (N=51)	Operators (N=19)	Laborers and Farm Workers (N=8)	Service Workers (N=34)
Career	70%	82%	60%	67%	47%	88%	65%
Family	11	7	16	12	11	13	18
Health	5	1	5	2	5	0	3
Religion	2	1	3	4	5	0	3
Leisure	7	5	9	16	16	0	9
Art	5	4	5	0	11	0	3
Citizenship	0	0	1	0	5	0	0

Table 46: Triggers for Learning by Occupation

Life Area of Trigger	Professional, Technical (N=128)	Managers, Officials (N=114)	Salesworkers, Clerical (N=92)	Craftsmen (N=51)	Operators (N=19)	Laborers and Farm Workers (N=8)	Service Workers (N=34)
Career	69%	79%	51%	71%	53%	50%	53%
Family	23	20	40	26	42	38	41
Health	6	0	5	0	0	13	3
Religion	2	1	1	4	0	0	3
Leisure	0	0	0	0	0	0	0
Art	0	0	0	0	0	0	0
Citizenship	0	0	2	0	5	0	0

Table 47: Number of Topics Studied in the Past 12 Months

Number of Topics	Learners in Transition (N = 616)	Learners Not in Transition (N = 128)	Total (N = 744)
1	41%	54%	43%
2	36	34	35
3	16	8	15
4	5	3	5
5	2	1	2
6	1	1	1

Table 48: Number of Topics Studied by Life Area of Transition

Number of Topics	Career (N=347)	Family (N=98)	Health (N=29)	Religion (N=23)	Leisure (N=79)	Art (N=32)	Citizenship (N=8)
1	50%	12%	76%	52%	32%	16%	50%
2	30	53	21	22	48	50	25
3	14	25	3	13	15	22	25
4	4	8	0	9	5	12	0
5	2	2	0	4	0	0	0
6	1	1	0	0	0	0	0

Table 49: Type of Topics Learned

Type of Topic	Learners in Transition (N = 616)	Learners Not in Transition (N = 128)	Total (N = 744)
Business administration/ management*	6%	0%	5%
Education*	3	2	3
Health care*	6	2	5
Office skills*	5	2	5
Skilled trades*	10	4	9
Other occupational courses*	11	4	10
Academic	7	6	7
Gardening/landscaping	5	5	5
Citizenship	0	1	0
Crafts	6	12	7
Fine arts	6	11	7
Family life	10	6	9
Leisure/sports/ physical fitness	7	10	8
Religion and ethics	7	31	11
Miscellaneous	11	5	10

* Topics related primarily to career preparation.

Table 50: Type of Topics Studied by Life Area of Transition

Type of Topic	Career (N=347)	Family (N=98)	Health (N=29)	Religion (N=23)	Leisure (N=79)	Art (N=32)	Citizenship (N=8)
Business administration/ management*	11%	0%	0%	0%	0%	0%	0%
Education*	5	2	0	0	0	0	0
Health care*	8	3	7	0	0	0	13
Office skills*	9	0	0	0	0	0	0
Skilled trades*	15	6	0	0	3	0	0
Other occupational courses*	18	3	0	0	4	3	0
Academic	8	5	3	0	9	0	25
Gardening/ landscaping	2	14	7	0	8	0	0
Citizenship	0	0	0	0	0	0	0
Crafts	1	2	3	4	22	38	25
Fine arts	1	0	17	0	9	59	0
Family life	3	45	3	0	5	0	25
Leisure/sports/ physical fitness	1	1	48	4	34	0	0
Religion and ethics	1	13	7	87	1	0	13
Miscellaneous	16	5	3	4	6	0	0

* Topics related primarily to career preparation.

Table 51: Location of Study*

Location of Study	Learners in Transition (N = 616)	Learners Not in Transition (N = 128)	Total (N = 744)
Completely on my own	27%	33%	28%
Private instruction	10	19	12
Local school district	7	7	7
Community/junior college	8	5	7
4-year university/college	15	11	14
Area vocational/technical institute	2	2	2
2-year technical institute	0	0	0
Proprietary	1	1	1
Voluntary/community agency or organization	5	4	5
Professional associations	4	1	4
Cultural institutions	0	1	0
Religious institutions	5	22	8
Employer	17	14	17
Union	0	0	0
Military service	0	0	0
Television station	1	1	1
Radio station	0	1	0
Newspaper	0	0	0
New type of college**	0	1	0
Correspondence school	1	1	1
Other	3	0	3

* Multiple responses account for column totals above 100%.
** Independent study under the direction of an instructor.

Table 52: Location of Study by Life Area of Transition*

Location of Study	Career (N=348)	Family (N=98)	Health (N=29)	Religion (N=23)	Leisure (N=79)	Art (N=32)	Citizenship (N=8)
Completely on my own	15%	53%	31%	43%	35%	41%	25%
Private instruction	3	14	10	9	29	38	0
Local school district	6	4	14	0	10	13	0
Community/ junior college	11	5	3	4	4	3	0
4-year college/ university	24	3	3	4	5	3	13
Area vocational/ technical school	3	3	3	0	1	0	0
2-year technical institute	1	0	0	0	0	0	0
Proprietary school	1	0	0	0	1	0	0
Voluntary/community agency or organization	1	2	28	0	11	6	25
Professional association	6	2	0	0	4	6	0
Cultural institutions	0	2	0	0	0	0	13
Religious institutions	1	9	3	65	1	3	0
Employer	27	5	3	0	0	0	13
Union	1	0	0	0	0	0	0
Military service	1	0	0	0	1	0	0
Television station	0	1	7	0	0	0	0
Radio station	0	0	0	4	0	0	0
Newspaper	0	1	3	0	1	0	0
New type of college**	0	0	0	0	0	0	0
Correspondence school	2	0	0	0	1	0	0
Other	3	3	3	0	0	0	13

* Multiple responses account for column totals above 100%.
** Independent study under the direction of an instructor.

APPENDIX B: METHODOLOGY

In this appendix, we discuss the design and procedures for carrying out the study detailed in *Americans in Transition*. The major topics addressed include choosing a methodological approach, selecting a population, selecting a sample, characteristics of the sample, developing the instrument, and conducting the interviews.

We might have chosen any one of several methods for investigating the hypothesis. Each possibility had something to recommend it as well as something to discourage it. Some of the options we considered—along with a discussion of why we might have used them and why we decided to reject them at this time—follow.

Choosing a Methodology

CASE STUDIES. Case studies are most useful when there is no clear hypothesis to guide the investigation. An in-depth examination of a few carefully selected cases can yield insights into each case, perhaps (if the investigator is lucky) generalizations across several cases, and hypotheses that the patterns observed in those cases appear at large in the society.

We rejected case studies because we already had a hypothesis drawn from our earlier investigations and we wanted to test it with a larger population. However, pilot testing the draft interview guide in face-to-face interviews with approximately 100 adults in five cities enabled us to build up a small file of "mini case studies" and allowed a small-scale verification of our hypothesis before undertaking the larger nationwide study.

INDIVIDUAL INTERVIEWS. There is no completely satisfactory substitute for an individual interview carried out by a skillful investigator who is an expert in the field. Such a person can go beyond any formal instrument—indeed, can use himself or herself as the "instrument" —and can follow leads in the conversation as they arise. Moreover, such a person can make better use of his or her background of training and experience to interpret the data having gathered its full nuances in the field.

However, the method is extremely expensive because of staff and travel costs. We rejected it because, while it would have produced extremely high-quality data, it would not have produced much data.

GROUP INTERVIEWS. The two primary advantages of group interviews are that they reduce the cost of each interview and allow the participants to be stimulated by each others' comments. Like individual interviews, they are most effective when conducted by skilled experts in the field. However, even though they cost less than individual interviews, they are considerably more expensive per respondent than certain other methods. We rejected group interviews in favor of less expensive techniques that would give us less data about more people.

MAILED QUESTIONNAIRES. One of the least expensive methods of collecting data—mailed questionnaires—yield more responses per $1,000 than most other methods. We seriously considered using questionnaires for that reason, but there are two problems with them. One, there is no interaction between investigator and respondent— the investigator cannot answer respondents' questions; cannot get them back on the track when they misunderstand the questionnaire. Second, there is response bias, the fact that some people do not answer and may differ systematically from those who do answer. It is difficult to identify response bias; it is more difficult to correct for it. Therefore, we rejected the use of mailed questionnaires.

TELEPHONE QUESTIONNAIRES. A middle ground between face-to-face interviews by experts and a massive number of mailed questionnaires is telephone questionnaires used by nonexperts. This procedure works best when the subject under investigation is thoroughly understood and when the data lend themselves to highly structured interview guides. The cost is relatively low when nonexperts are used.

Moreover, telephone calls allow a certain amount of probing to get relevant answers and to verify them, as well as a chance to clarify respondents' questions and to keep their answers on track, although having nonexperts make the telephone calls loses some of that advantage.

We decided to use telephone questionnaires administered by non-experts as the method that would give us a large number of interviews at low cost. While our understanding of the subject was not good enough to allow highly structured questions on every topic, that shortcoming was what offset the fact that the telephone survey allowed some interaction between interviewers and respondents.

Selecting a Population

There were at least three possible choices as to which population to investigate: (1) adults currently engaged in learning, including those enrolled in formal educational institutions and/or those engaged in some kind of informal or independent study; (2) adult learners at large in the society, including those learning both currently and recently; and (3) nonlearning adults at large in the society.

The advantage of the first choice would have been the accurate identification of actual adult learners (as opposed to those who might only claim to be learning) as well as having those adult learners neatly divided according to type of educational institution. That approach would have guaranteed that every interview would be with a valid case of a learning adult, with no time wasted dealing with nonlearners.

The disadvantages would have been considerable expense and traveling to a cross-section of institutions to conduct the interviews and the lack of any adult nonlearners to compare and contrast with the learners. We rejected that population because the disadvantages outweighed the advantages.

The advantages of the second choice were that we could reach adults engaged in informal or independent learning as well as those enrolled in formal courses, could get a more representative sample at the same cost, and could collect a certain amount of comparative data from nonlearners at the same time. The disadvantages of this choice were locating and talking with many nonlearners, reducing the number of learners we could interview, and permitting some unknown fraction of the respondents to claim they were learning when in fact they were not. We chose this population because we thought the advantages outweighed the disadvantages.

The primary advantage of the third choice is that it would open the possibility of gaining insights into why adults do not learn. That approach had a certain appeal. Many adults are not learning. Therefore, we could have investigated the question: What causes adults not to seek learning? Some members of our advisory panel urged us to do exactly that: examine nonlearning and try to explain it.

The concept of studying nonbehavior seemed to us not only methodologically difficult, but theoretically unpromising. Consequently, we decided not to study nonlearning, but simply to collect the demographic characteristics of adult nonlearners to see if they differed in some systematic way from adult learners. We hypothesized that they would not, as previous studies had already indicated.

Selecting a Sample

The design of the study called for a nationally representative sample of adults 25 years of age or older, including part-time and full-time students. The sample was to represent the general population of the United States according to geographic region, age, sex, marital status, education, employment status, and occupation.

A sample size of approximately 1,500 adults was determined to be sufficient to project, for the nation as a whole, the percentage of learners to nonlearners and to provide an adequate sample of each group on which to base the findings of the study. This figure was based on an initial pilot test, which revealed that the percentage of learners was approximately 50 percent. That being the case, the number of learners and nonlearners that would result from a sample of 1,500 persons would be approximately 750 for each group.

The sample was drawn from a national probability sample of telephone households across 200 primary sampling units (PSUs).[1] These 200 PSUs were drawn across nine geographic regions in the United States. (Results reported in "Part II: Findings" confirm good representation of the study sample across these nine regions.) Random digit dialing was the method chosen over listed telephone dialing because it reaches an additional 23 percent of the population (8 percent of the population with private, unlisted numbers and 15 percent of the population who have recently moved and are "between telephones"). Thirty telephone numbers were generated randomly by the computer for each PSU, yielding a total of 6,000 numbers.

Based on prior nationwide studies where a random digit dialing

---

1. A primary sampling unit in this study is a county or group of contiguous counties.

approach was used and based on the response rate of learners to non-learners in initial pilot tests, it was determined that the 6,000 or so random numbers would produce approximately 1,500 adults representing the characteristics of the nation's population reported earlier.

Characteristics of the Sample

The 1,519 adults 25 years of age or older who responded to the telephone survey were distributed across the nation's nine geographic regions precisely in the way that the nation's population is distributed.[2] That is, the geographic representativeness of the survey sample is excellent (Table 53).

The ages of respondents were a close match to the ages of the population nationwide (Table 54). Females were slightly more numerous than males among the survey respondents, just as is the case with the national population (Table 55).

The marital status of the respondents was reasonably close to that for adults nationwide, except that the survey sample contained somewhat fewer married persons and somewhat more single and widowed persons. These differences are not due to any age bias in the sample (Table 56).

The respondents were considerably better educated than the population as a whole, although the typical respondent, like the typical adult, held a high school diploma. The survey sample contained an unusually high proportion of college-educated persons (about 50 percent more than in the general population) and an unusually low proportion of persons with less than a high school education (about 35 percent fewer than in the general population) (Table 57).

The employment status of respondents paralleled almost exactly that for the nation as a whole. That is, the percent employed full-time and part-time, the percent unemployed, and the percent who are homemakers or retired is virtually identical to that for the nation (Table 58).

Although an equal proportion was employed, the survey respondents held somewhat higher-level jobs than other adults. The respondents included more professional and technical workers and

---

2. All comparisons to the nation's population are based on data from the U.S. Bureau of the Census, *Current Population Reports,* and the U.S. Bureau of Labor Statistics, *Employment and Earnings,* 1977.

almost twice as many managers, proprietors, and officials as the total population but, conversely, the respondents included fewer operators, laborers, farmers, and service workers (Table 59).

Developing the Instrument

The study questionnaire gathered data on whether the respondent was learning, what was being learned where, and most important, what types of transitions caused such learning. A number of demographic items were included in order to profile both learners and nonlearners. In addition, the questionnaire gathered information on how adults spend their time in a typical week.

Several steps were taken to develop the questionnaire. First, a careful analysis was performed of existing state and local surveys of adult learners (of which there are approximately 30), surveys conducted on adult learning nationwide (including NCES Triennial surveys, Carp, Peterson, and Roelfs survey of 1972, etc.), and surveys conducted by the College Board, such as that used for *Forty Million Americans in Career Transition.*

Second, in order to identify the types of transitions most appropriate to our hypothesis and to develop questions and techniques to elicit "trigger" events that have caused learning, more than 100 interviews were conducted face-to-face in five cities across the country: Atlanta, Boston, Chicago, Dallas, and San Francisco. In each city, a representative sample of adult learners, 25 years of age and older, was recruited and interviewed for approximately 45 minutes. In this period of time, questions aimed at determining whether life transitions triggered the learning being discussed were generated and tested. Thus, through the face-to-face interview approach, both the hypothesis regarding transitions and triggers as well as techniques for posing the questions were resolved.

Third, the questionnaire covering more than 20 topics was prepared for pilot testing by telephone. The pilot test was conducted with approximately 50 randomly selected adults. On the basis of the pilot test, the 20 or so items were revised and perfected. The questionnaire was administered to 1,500 adults and took approximately 30 minutes to complete.

Conducting the Interviews

Valley Forge Information Service (VFIS), a centralized long-distance WATS line interviewing service, was selected by the College Board to conduct the telephone interviews. VFIS is an independent, full-service market research company located in Valley Forge, Pennsylvania. VFIS assumed full responsibility for drawing the sample of adults from its national probability sample, assisted in the technical design of the survey instrument, participated in the pilot testing of the survey instrument, and trained the more than 30 interviewers who conducted the 1,500 or so interviews. The success of VFIS in reaching the 1,500 adults is described in this section.

Reaching 1,500 Adults

Approximately 5,000 telephone numbers (of the 6,000 generated) were dialed in order to reach the desired sample of approximately 1,500 adults. The following chart indicates the breakdown of all numbers dialed, resulting in the desired sample size.

```
Total number of telephone numbers: ..................... 4,997
Less nonhouseholds
  A. Nonworking numbers.................... 1,795
  B. Nonhouseholds ........................   261    2,056
     Households in sample ........................... 2,941
Results of calls to households:
  Refused............................................    479
  Nonavailability of selected respondent (3 callbacks)......   163
  Language barrier......................................     85
  Ineligible (because of age)...........................    101
  No answer/busy (3 callbacks).........................    573
  Illness ..............................................     21
  Total................................................  1,519
    A. Learners .......................................    744
    B. Nonlearners....................................    775
```

The approach used by VFIS in randomly selecting an adult in each household contacted was as follows. First, when contact was made with a household, the initial respondent was asked to list all adults in the household 25 years of age or older. From the list of all those listed in each household, the VFIS interviewer, using a preexisting table of random numbers, selected one person in the household with whom to conduct the interview. If it happened to be the initial respondent, the interview was conducted immediately (or at a later time convenient to the respondent). If the interview was to be conducted with someone else in the household, a day and time were recorded for calling back. Three callbacks were allowed in order to reach a potential respondent. If that respondent could not be reached after three calls, then his/her name was dropped and replaced.

Table 53: Region — Comparison of Respondents to Census

Region	1977 U.S. Census* (N = 124 million)	College Board Study Respondents (N = 1,519)
New England	6%	5%
Middle Atlantic	18	18
South Atlantic	16	16
East South Central	6	7
West South Central	10	10
East North Central	19	20
West North Central	8	8
Mountain	4	4
Pacific	14	14

* Current Population Reports, Population Characteristics Series P-20, U.S. Department of Commerce, Bureau of the Census.

Table 54: Age — Comparison of Respondents to Census

Years	1978 U.S. Census* (N = 126 million)	College Board Study Respondents (N = 1,519)
25 – 29	14%	16%
30 – 34	13	13
35 – 44	19	20
45 – 54	18	18
55 – 64	16	15
65 and over	19	14

* Current Population Reports, Population Estimates and Projections, Series P-25, No. 800, Issued April 1979: Estimates of the population of the United States by age, sex, and race: 1976 to 1978. Table 2 Estimates of the Resident Population of the United States, by Age, Sex, and Race: July 1, 1976 to 1978 (TN-126,996).

Table 55: Sex — Comparison of Respondents to Census

Sex	1978 U.S. Census* (N = 126 million)	College Board Study Respondents (N = 1,519)
Male	47%	49%
Female	53	51

* Current Population Reports, Population Characteristics, Series P-20, No. 338. Issued May 1979: Marital Status and Living Arrangements: March 1978. Table 1. Marital Status by Age, Race and Spanish Origin, Farm and Nonfarm Residence and Sex. This report excludes inmates of institutions. It includes 874,000 members of the armed forces in 1978 who were living off post or with their families on post but excludes all other members of the armed forces.

Table 56: Marital Status — Comparison of Respondents to Census

Marital Status	1978 U.S. Census* (N = 126 million)	College Board Study Respondents (N = 1,519)
Married	71%	68%
Divorced/separated	10	9
Widowed	10	13
Never married/single	9	11

* Current Population Reports, Population Characteristics, Series P-20, No. 338. Issued May 1979: Marital Status and Living Arrangements: March 1978. Table 1. Marital Status by Age, Race and Spanish Origin, Farm and Nonfarm Residence and Sex. This report excludes inmates of institutions. It includes 874,000 members of the armed forces in 1978 who were living off post or with their families on post but excludes all other members of the armed forces.

Table 57: Education — Comparison of Respondents to Census

Education	1977 U.S. Census* (N = 124 million)	College Board Study Respondents (N = 1,519)
8 years of school or less	20%	11%
1-3 years of high school	15	12
High school diploma	36	35
Some college	13	20
4-year college degree or more	15	22

* Current Population Reports, Population Characteristics, Series P-20, No. 314. Educational Attainment in the United States: March 1977 and 1976. Issued December 1977.

Table 58: Employment Status — Comparison of Respondents to Census

Employment Status	1979 U.S. Census* (N = 128 million)	College Board Study Respondents (N = 1,519)
Employed (net)	66%	62%
Full-time	59	56
Part-time	7	6
Unemployed	3	4
Other (Retired, homemaker, or student)	34	33

* United States Bureau of Labor Statistics, unpublished data.

Table 59: Occupation — Comparison of Respondents to Census

Occupation	1978 U.S. Census* (N = 86 million)	College Board Study Respondents (N = 942)
Professional, technical, and kindred	16%	21%
Managers, proprietors, and officials	12	23
Salesworkers, clerical, and kindred	24	21
Craftsmen	14	16
Operators	15	7
Laborer, except farm	4	2
Farmer, farm worker	3	1
Service worker	12	9

* Employment and Earning. 1978 Annual Averages, U.S. Department of Labor, Bureau of Labor Statistics, January 1979. Table 21. Employed Persons by Occupation, Sex, and Age (Ages 20 and Over).

WHAT IS FDLS?

The Future Directions for a Learning Society (FDLS) Program is a major effort toward the realization of a learning society in the United States. The program focuses on improving access and transition for learners, which has been the College Board's role in education for more than 75 years. By building on recent Board programs that have increasingly focused on adults, the program extends this historic role to include assistance to adult learners and to the diverse agencies, institutions, and organizations that provide learning opportunities for them.

Funded by the Exxon Education Foundation, FDLS develops consensus and support for strategies, services, and policies that can best meet current and projected needs of participants and providers in a learning society. To this end, the program solicits and relies on the participation of professional people in the field, public policymakers, and the larger community. A major purpose of the Exxon grant is to promote the mobilization of additional funds and other resources necessary for major initiatives in this developing field. The initial grant supports the project's planning and management, the identification and design of service areas, the review and analysis of public policy, and publishing of relevant materials.

The program produces projections of future trends, information about the needs of learners and providers of educational opportunities and resources, policy recommendations, and services. The program is engaged in finding better ways to gauge the needs of learners, in identifying the problems institutions face in meeting learners' needs, in strengthening learning opportunities, and in increasing public, professional, and political understanding of the field. A chief focus of the program is to demonstrate promising new approaches and specific services.

OTHER PUBLICATIONS FROM FUTURE DIRECTIONS FOR A LEARNING SOCIETY

Adult Access to Education and New Careers: A Handbook for Action Carol B. Aslanian, Project Director; Harvey B. Schmelter, Editor. 1980. 142 pages. (001257) $9.75.

Expand Your Life: A Pocket Book for Personal Change Allen Tough. 1980. 64 pages. (001249) $2.50.

The Federal Role in Lifelong Learning Ellen Hoffman. 1980. 32 pages. (237413) $3.

40 Million Americans in Career Transition: The Need for Information Solomon Arbeiter, Carol B. Aslanian, Frances A. Schmerbeck, Henry M. Brickell. 1978. 55 pages. (237403) $4.50.

Learning Times 1979. 12 pages. (248100) $7.50 per 50 copies; available in multiples of 50. No further discounts apply.

Linking the Worker to Postsecondary Education: A Manual for Training Study Organizers in America Harvey B. Schmelter. 1980. 112 pages. (237415) $9.75.

The Missing Link: Connecting Adult Learners to Learning Resources K. Patricia Cross. 1978. 80 pages. (237402) $4.50.

Participation and Persistence in American Adult Education: Implications for Public Policy in Future Research from a Multivariate Analysis of a National Data Base   Richard E. Anderson and Gordon G. Darkenwald. 1979. 42 pages. (237404) $3.

Paying for Your Education: A Guide for Adult Learners   1980. 72 pages. (001265) Single copy, $3.50; 100-999 copies, $1 each; 1,000-9,999 copies, 75¢ each; 10,000 copies or more, 50¢ each.

Planning for a Statewide Educational Information Center Network   William D. Van Dusen, Ronald H. Miller, Donna M. Pokorny. 1978. 33 pages. (237406) Single copy, $3.50; 5-24 copies, $2.80 each; 25 or more, $2 each.

Telephone Counseling for Home-Based Adults   Solomon Arbeiter, Carol B. Aslanian, Frances A. Schmerbeck, Henry M. Brickell. 1978. 65 pages. (237405) $4.50.

350 Ways Colleges Are Serving Adult Learners   1979. 47 pages. (237410) $2.

To order these publications, send payment or institutional purchase order to:
College Board Publication Orders
Box 2815
Princeton, New Jersey 08541